THE OPEN UNIVERSITY

An Arts Foundation Course
Units 3, 4 and 5

Introduction to History

Prepared by Arthur Marwick for the Course Team

The Open University Press

Front cover   Stratford-upon-Avon's first borough charter of 1553.
Back cover   Top left: Gare du Nord, Paris (French Railways Ltd)
Top right: Mylne's Court, Lawnmarket, Edinburgh (Scottish Tourist Board, Edinburgh)
Bottom left: Shakespeare's birthplace, Stratford-upon-Avon (Herald Photographic Services, Stratford-upon-Avon)
Bottom right: St Pancras Station, London

The Open University Press
Walton Hall, Milton Keynes
MK7 6AA

First published 1977

Designed by the Media Development Group of the Open University.

Printed in Great Britain by
EYRE AND SPOTTISWOODE LIMITED
AT GROSVENOR PRESS PORTSMOUTH

ISBN 0 335 05411 0

This text forms part of an Open University course. The complete list of units in the course appears at the end of this text.

For general availability of supporting material referred to in this text, please write to Open University Educational Enterprises Limited, 12 Cofferidge Close, Stony Stratford, Milton Keynes, MK11 1BY, Great Britain.

Further information on Open University courses may be obtained from the Admissions Office, The Open University, P.O. Box 48, Walton Hall, Milton Keynes, MK7 6AB.

1.1

CONTENTS   INTRODUCTION TO HISTORY

PREFACE

In this three-week block, we turn to a discussion of the aims and methods of one single humanities discipline, history.

The approach may be very different from anything you have learned or picked up previously about the study of history. We shall not be specially concerned with particular facts about particular periods in the past; we are concerned with the methods of history, how the historian goes about his tasks, how to distinguish good history from bad history, how you yourself should read history, and how you should write your own history essays. To make this study more manageable, and to make it easier to include cross-references from the other humanities, I shall draw many of my examples from the period of the European Renaissance (broadly, the fourteenth, fifteenth and sixteenth centuries). And since the course ends with an extended study, *Arts and Society in an Age of Industrialization*, which covers industrialization in nineteenth-century Britain, I shall also draw some examples from that period. But there will also be references to other periods in history, and to the present. I hope you will learn a little bit about the Renaissance and a little bit at this stage about industrialization, but that is not the main point of this part of the course. Our concern is with the methods, the purposes, and the techniques of history, not with particular historical periods or topics.

AIMS

The overall aims of these units are:

1   To encourage you to see history as a *relevant* subject and as a valuable introduction to the *varieties* of human experience.

2   To help you to appreciate that history, on the one hand, is a serious discipline with a rigorous methodology, while, on the other hand, it is not a mere matter of 'ascertaining the facts', but involves a high degree of interpretive, and indeed, creative imagination.

3   To awaken you to the richness and complexity of primary source material.

4   To introduce you to some of the fundamental problems involved in the handling of source material.

5   To make you aware of how history is written.

6   To provide the basic criteria upon which you can assess the relative merits of different secondary authorities.

7   By explaining basic principles and exposing the more obvious pitfalls (for example periodization, semantics, imprecision) to guide you towards intelligent historical composition of your own.

8   To enable you to discuss critically how far, and in what senses, history can set the temporal and social context for the other humanities and to discuss the relationships between history and the other humanities' disciplines.

OBJECTIVES

Introduction to History is divided into three units, each unit being equivalent to one week's work. Sections within units are numbered 1, 2 etc. Each section sets out to achieve one basic objective, and (although different students will inevitably work at different speeds) should involve roughly three-quarters of an hour's work; some sections of course may take longer, some are shorter. Where the material is completely new to you, you may have to read it several times before you grasp it fully. Please take the self-assessment exercises very seriously, keeping my specimen answers covered, while you write your own answers in your notebooks.

Here now is a complete plan of the three units. Detailed objectives will be given at the beginning of each unit, when the titles of the sections are listed followed by the objectives of each section. The idea of listing objectives in this way is for you to see what you are expected to be able to do at the end of each section. Once you have completed the entire three weeks' work you should then, ideally, be in a position to achieve the eight general aims listed above. However, *Introduction to History* is not totally self-contained. It forms only a small section of this entire multi-disciplinary foundation course. We have designed the course so that your work will be cumulative. At the end of the three weeks you may well not be fully satisfied that you have achieved all of the objectives or all of the aims. But as you proceed in the course you will find that what you have learned here relates to what you will learn in later blocks; and points which you did not fully understand, or whose significance you are not clear about, will gradually fit into place as you work your way through the course. It is in the final third of the course *Arts and Society in an Age of Industrialization* that the history aims and objectives should fully merge with all the other disciplines enabling you to achieve the aims set out for the course as a whole.

PLAN OF THE THREE UNITS

Unit 3   The Significance of History

This unit discusses the reasons for studying history, what history is about, the way the study of history has developed (particularly since the early nineteenth century), and questions how far historical writing is necessarily biased, how far it is scientific, etc.

Unit 4   Primary Sources

All serious historical scholarship is based on the study of primary sources. This unit discusses the nature and range of primary sources and the critical techniques which the historian brings to bear on them, and how he turns them into historical writing.

Unit 5   The Writing of History

This unit discusses in detail the problems of writing history both as encountered by the professional historian and by you as a student. It suggests some of the ways in which you can distinguish between good historical writing and bad historical writing. In the final section the unit relates history to the other humanities' disciplines.

SET BOOKS

Your next three weeks' work, then, consists of working your way through these three units, in conjunction of course with the radio and television programmes. You will need to have beside you the main set book for this part of the course, A. G. Dickens, *The Age of Humanism and Reformation*; you will also need the Course Reader, *Nature and Industrialization*[1] and the Supplementary Texts.

Ideally you should have already read *The Age of Humanism and Reformation* through at least once, since it is on the recommended list of preliminary reading.

[1] Alasdair Clayre (ed) (1977) *Nature and Industrialization*, Oxford University Press/The Open University Press.

For preliminary reading you were also referred to my book *The Nature of History*. As *The Age of Humanism and Reformation* itself involves quite a heavy burden of reading, *The Nature of History* is no longer a set book (as it was in the original version of the Arts Foundation Course). However, you may well still find it useful background reading for following up many of the points which I simply do not have space to deal with fully in these units, and I have included some references to it which, however, are very much optional extras. (If you *are* interested, the simplest method would probably be to look up all the references to *The Nature of History* at the end of each week's work.)

Reading, and profiting from, books of the quality of *The Age of Humanism and Reformation* is one of the skills you must develop as a humanities student. If you are totally new to academic work you may well find it quite hard going to begin with. Unit 3 seeks to help you to understand what history is and how it is written: but you can only fully grasp the message by reading, and digesting, for yourself a real piece of first-class historical writing. That is the first reason why it is essential for you to read this book; the second reason is that it provides the necessary context of Renaissance history to help you to make cross-disciplinary references between the other humanities you will be studying, and history.

I shall set exercises which direct you to particular parts of *The Age of Humanism and Reformation*, but you must at this stage come to grips with the problem of carrying on independent reading apart from the course material itself. Since the book is your own, there is no harm in using a pencil to annotate passages which particularly strike you: this will certainly help to concentrate your mind on your reading. As you work through my correspondence material you will learn more and more of what to look for in an historical work of this sort. But as I say, you have to start sometime, so if you feel you need the guidance, I suggest the following tentative reading plan:

1   *Before* starting on Unit 3 read Chapter One (and note, if you are puzzled, that *Quattrocento* – 'four hundred' in Italian – means what we call the fifteenth century).

2   Before finishing Unit 3 (I suggest between my sections 4 and 5) read *at least* section 1 of Chapter Two (I hope you will read the whole of these chapters, but if you are pushed for time this is the minimum necessary *meantime*).

3   Before starting Unit 4 read *at least* sections 4 and 5 of Chapter Three and sections 1, 4 and 5 of Chapter Four.

4   Before starting Unit 5 read *at least* section 2 of Chapter Five.

5   You will need to read section 5 of Chapter Five in connection with Unit 5, section 2, and the Postscript in connection with Unit 5, section 4.

But let me repeat that this plan is provided only in case you find difficulty in getting the minimum necessary work done in the time at your disposal. I very much hope that you will be able to enjoy reading *The Age of Humanism and Reformation* in its entirety in a more relaxed way.

Experience shows that many of you will have difficulty in finding your way through what at first will seem like a bewildering array of new information and new concepts in *The Age of Humanism and Reformation*. To repeat: the two main reasons for getting you to read this book are:

1   To enable you to explore the techniques of historical writing at its best. Later in the units you will find exercises which require you to draw upon this book; obviously the further ahead you get with your reading, the more sense these exercises will make when you read them.

2   To provide you with detailed knowledge of the Renaissance period. In part, you will be able to use *The Age of Humanism and Reformation* as a reference book at, for example, summer school. But meantime, to help you in your general reading through the book I am providing here a very simplified

checklist of the main developments which (in my view at least!) go to make up the Renaissance period. As you read through Dickens see where, and how, the things he is saying match up with, and amplify, the points on my checklist. For example, the whole opening discussion of humanism ties up directly with my point 1. Then at the foot of page 5 and top of page 6 he is in effect dealing with my point 2. On page 37 he qualifies my perhaps over-simplified point 10. And so on. If you keep my checklist beside you, and keep making comments of this sort, you will (I hope!) find an overall picture of the Renaissance period emerging more clearly – and that is what I want you to get from your reading.

Checklist of main developments making up the Renaissance period

1 First of all there was the turning among intellectuals towards the classical wisdom of Ancient Greece and Ancient Rome. This is the absolute fundamental of the Renaissance as an intellectual and artistic movement. But this turning to the past had a liberating effect which led to discoveries and changes which went beyond the wisdom of the classics.

2 Springing out of this, but linked also to the other changes, was a change in the way in which men thought about society and the world in which they lived, involving: (a) a new emphasis on man as a comprehensible being worthy of study, and on his real needs as distinct from the overarching theological concepts of the middle ages; and (b) a change from the contemplative, passive, 'monastic' spirit to one which encouraged men to take an active part in economic and political life.

3 Again linked to both of these, we have the great changes in the styles of artistic and literary expression, so clearly seen in the great painters of the Italian Renaissance, and also in the plays of Shakespeare.

4 Thinking men of the time were actually aware of these intellectual and artistic changes, and themselves, one way or another, spoke of 'a Renaissance'. This belief, among intellectuals, is a special characteristic of the age.

5 Fifthly (and from the point of view of whole societies perhaps most significantly), there was a great expansion in trade and commerce, together with great changes and upheavals in the social structures of the various European countries: expressing this in a very shorthand fashion, one can say that feudalism slowly gave way to capitalism.

6 There were important technological developments, and a development of a whole new scientific outlook.

7 The rapid spread of printing (invented in the fifteenth century) the great increase in lay education, and the widespread use of the vernacular languages (instead of Latin) added up to a great expansion in the possibilities of *communication*.

8 The fifteenth century onwards marked the beginning of the great age of European exploration and colonization.

9 A great split in Christendom took place in the early sixteenth century, followed by a long period of religious wars, and religious controversy.

10 There were important political changes: the Turkish Empire emerged as a major Eastern Empire; above all, the nation state (best exemplified by France and England) now began to take its place as the most important political unit in modern European history.

ASSIGNMENTS

At the end of Unit 5 you should do the assignment. This assignment plays a particularly important role in helping you develop the general skills of writing, apart altogether from its specifically historical function.

EXERCISES

I have already mentioned the exercises which are designed to test whether you are actually achieving the objectives of the individual sections. It is very important that you make a genuine effort to answer the questions before turning to my specimen answers and discussions. On the other hand, if you find yourself getting really stuck, then there is nothing wrong in proceeding to my answers. My purpose, as it were, is to try to enter into a 'discussion' with you. The main point is that you should understand my discussions and my reasons for regarding some answers as 'wrong' and others as 'correct' (perhaps I should really say: more nearly 'correct' or more probably 'correct') and therefore preferring the latter. Often, because the humanities are like that, there will be no one absolutely 'correct' answer. Sometimes in my answers I will add extra pieces of information which you could not possibly have been expected to put in your own answers. Do not be upset by this: just imagine that you are in a tutorial discussion with me and that I have gone on to make some points which you may find interesting, but which I do not expect you to memorize.

The answers you write to these exercises are for your eyes alone: you are not in any way going to be assessed on them. Some of the exercises may seem very simple, some of them quite difficult. Sometimes you will find it necessary to refer back to earlier parts of the correspondence material in order to give an intelligent answer to the question. Let me repeat that the idea is to try to get you into some kind of *discussion* with me; I want you to think about the various problems put to you in the exercises. Your continuous assessment (which will contribute to your final result at the end of the whole course) will be based on the tutor-marked assignments which you return to us. The more genuine the attempt you have made at the exercises, the better you are likely to do in the assignments.

RADIO AND TELEVISION PROGRAMMES

Before listening to, or viewing, the radio and television programmes associated with each unit, you should have studied the relevant broadcast notes, which will make clear any preparation necessary to get the best value out of the programme.

Television programme 3, *Writing history*, relates to Unit 3 in so far as it serves to introduce the purpose and excitement of historical research and writing. It also serves to prepare you for the detailed work on the writing of history in Unit 5; and there is a reference to it in Unit 4.

Radio programme 3, *Radio history: an exercise in constructive criticism*, is also concerned with the excitement of historical study, but its main purpose is to introduce you to the sort of critical methods you are asked to develop throughout these three units.

Both television programme 4, *Primary sources*, and radio programme 4, *Handling primary sources*, accompanying Unit 4 deal with primary sources and the critical techniques the historian brings to bear on them.

In accordance with the general broadcasting pattern adopted for this foundation course television programme 5, *Edinburgh observed*, and radio programme 5, *Art and the historian*, look out from history to another arts discipline – in both cases art history. They therefore relate to the final section of Unit 5. The radio programme also helps to introduce you more closely to Professor A. G. Dickens.

UNIT 3 THE SIGNIFICANCE OF HISTORY

CONTENTS

OBJECTIVES OF EACH SECTION

Section 1   Definitions

You should understand that the word 'history' is used in various different ways: the 'history' we are mainly concerned with is 'the historian's attempt to reconstruct and interpret the past', not 'the past' itself. You should be able to distinguish between the different uses of the word 'history'.

Section 2   Justifications for the Study of History

You should be able to list the various justifications which can be given for studying history. Beyond that you should familiarize yourself with the idea that history is a *social necessity* – the idea that history is as necessary to man and society as memory is to the individual, that without history man and society would be totally disorientated, would have no real sense of identity. You do not have to agree with this justification, but you should be able to argue about it.

Section 3   The Basic Concerns of the Historian

You should have mastered the idea, as a starting point for your historical studies, that the three basic concerns of the historian are:
(a) man in society;
(b) change through time;
      and
(c) particular unique events.
You should also understand that history involves *explanation* and the study of the *interconnections* between events: *history* should be distinguished from *chronicle* – mere narration of events without explanation or interpretation. You should therefore be able to distinguish history from other types of writing which occasionally bring in the past, such as sociology, political science, biology, astronomy, etc.

Section 4   The Subjective Element in History

You should understand why it is that although the historian should try to be as objective as he can, it is never completely possible to suppress personal and subjective elements in history. You should understand why it is that history must always in some sense be, as E. H. Carr has said, a 'dialogue between the present and the past': that is, in reconstructing and interpreting the past the historian is always influenced by the attitudes and prejudices of the age and society in which he lives.

Section 5   The Development of the Modern Discipline of History

You should know the names of, and the main achievements associated with, some of the really outstanding historians in the last two hundred years. You should understand how in the twentieth century there has emerged the concept of 'total history' – that is, history which looks at man's past in all its aspects, cultural and social, as well as economic and political.

Section 6   History as Science, History as Art, History as Art and Science

You should understand the various basic arguments which are put forward on the different sides of this quite difficult problem. You should be able to reach some conclusions of your own about how far history is scientific, how far it is an art.

1 DEFINITIONS

My colleague, Oswald Hanfling, tells me that it is often disastrous to start off with definitions. Still, I do think we must get clear in our minds what we mean by 'history'. If you reflect for a few moments you will realize that we use the word 'history' in various different ways.

Basically 'history' has two separate meanings. First of all it can be used to mean everything which actually happened in the past, whether this has been recorded by anyone or not. This usage is implied in a phrase such as 'history, if we could only know it all, would reveal the thoughts of God', or, more simply, 'what happened in history'. It would probably save some trouble if for this meaning we used the word 'the past'. But the fact is that single words are often used to cover different meanings. Since there is nothing we can do about it, the thing is to be clear about which meaning is intended.

The second meaning of 'history' is the history which has been recorded, the history which we actually know. Again, after a few moments' reflection, you will realize that this history can only be known through the activity of the person recording it, that is to say the historian.

There is then this basic distinction: between history as 'the past' and history as 'the historian's attempt to reconstruct that past'.

Looking closely at the second meaning we can make a further division of it. In far-off centuries many writers, poets, singers, made some effort to reconstruct the past, but often without any very positive attempt to distinguish between fact and myth. It is only in the last 200 years that history has been developed as a scholarly discipline. Apart then from history as (1) the past, the two other meanings of 'history' are:

2   the general attempt made by man throughout the centuries to describe, reconstruct, interpret the past which has been going on for centuries and continues today;

3   the attempt to do this in a scholarly fashion, sticking to certain definite rules of establishing fact, interpreting evidence, dealing with source material, etc.

In this course we are concerned with the last meaning, history as a discipline. But one of the complicated things is that it is not always possible, or even desirable, to make a rigid distinction between these last two kinds of history. We would not deny the title 'historian' to many of the figures of the past, from Thucydides, the ancient Greek historian, Bede the eighth-century English historian, to Voltaire and Gibbon the great eighteenth-century historians, all of whom were practising their craft before the modern discipline of history had begun to develop. (If you would like to check up on Thucydides, Bede, Voltaire and Gibbon, you can look them up in *The Nature of History*.)

EXERCISE

Listed below are various phrases involving different usages of the word 'history'. Identify which meaning is involved by entering:

A   to indicate history as 'the past'.

B   to indicate 'the general attempt made by man throughout the centuries to describe, reconstruct, interpret the past which has been going on for centuries and continues today'.

C   for history the academic discipline.
(If you are in doubt as between *B* and *C*, use *B*. Enter *C* only if you are absolutely certain that history as the academic discipline is clearly implied.)

1 Definitions

1 'History should always be taught in the Faculty
  of Arts not in the Faculty of Sciences.'

☐

2 'That television programme was very good as
  history.'

☐

3 'He preferred reading history to reading poetry.'

☐

4 'He preferred history to football.'

☐

5 'History is not the work of great men alone.'

☐

6 'Strictly speaking history is not a science.'

☐

7 'Economic influences determine the course of
  history, not political ones.'

☐

8 'We have had too much "drum-and-trumpet"
  history.'

☐

9 'History is bunk.'

☐

ANSWERS

1	C	4	B	7	A		
2	B	5	A	8	B		
3	B	6	C	9	B		

DISCUSSION

Remember the really important distinction is between A (history as the past) on the one side, and B and C (history as the historian's activity, whether scholarly or not, on the other). If at your first attempt you did not get the Bs and Cs properly sorted out this does not matter too much. But if you have *not* put an A for 5 and 7 or if you *have* put an A for any of the others, read the next five paragraphs, then go back and read the preceding correspondence material again.

Unless 5 is meant to mean 'not all *historians* are great men' – and if the writer had meant this, he presumably would have said so – 'history' here must mean the entire past.

Seven refers to the past as it happened – not to the historian's reconstruction of the past – though if the historian believed this statement to be true undoubtedly *he* would be influenced in the manner in which he writes about the past.

Three might possibly be C rather than B, though since history is being compared to poetry, the activity of the poet, rather than to the discipline of literature, it seems reasonable to think that history in the broader sense is intended here. In the case of 4 it is more difficult to tell whether meaning B or C is intended, so that, in strict accordance with my 'instructions', B is the correct answer. With regard to 6, C, history the discipline, is implied. There would be little point in telling us that history in the broad sense, history without claim to exact scholarly method, is not a science.

14

The author of 8 (J. R. Green – you can look him up in *The Nature of History* if you are interested) actually meant the history of professional historians (C), but again the statement could apply to *B*, which, therefore, is the 'correct' answer (but you did well if you said *C*). Henry Ford (the famous author of 9) also probably meant the history of the professionals; but the professional historian (naturally) would probably argue that the remark is only applicable to unscholarly history. It would, of course, be nonsense to say 'The past is bunk'.

If you are still puzzled go back and once again read carefully through the correspondence material. Before proceeding be sure that you have grasped this business of the different definitions of history.

2 JUSTIFICATIONS FOR THE STUDY OF HISTORY

In studying any subject it is important to have some idea of the aims and purposes of that subject, even if in the end you reject these aims and purposes. From now on when we talk of 'history' we will be thinking only of the second and third meanings of the word, that is to say we are basically concerned with history as an academic discipline, but we are recognizing too that an important form of history existed before the development of modern historical scholarship, and that many people keep up a genuine interest in history even though they are not professional scholars or teachers of history.

In my book *The Nature of History*, I describe history as a *social necessity*. Perhaps I was using words a trifle loosely. My point (which, of course, you may disagree with) is that no society can get along without a knowledge of its history. This, certainly, would explain why there have been historians right back to the earliest human societies, long before there was any academic study of history. Bards, witch doctors, troubadours, folk singers, griots (in West Africa), poets – anyone responsible for preserving and recounting stories of the past activities and triumphs of any particular tribe or society – are, in a rough way, historians practising history in the sense defined in the preceding exercise as *B* (p. 13). The argument here is that all human communities need the activities of such 'historians'. History is to the community, as memory is to the individual. Typically in everyday life and in novels and films, a man suffering from loss of memory is in a very tricky situation indeed. He finds great difficulty in adjusting himself to other people, in finding his bearings, in taking intelligent decisions about anything; he has lost his *sense of identity*. A society without history is in a similar condition. In fact the simplest answer to the question often asked (particularly by bored students of history): 'What is the use of history?' is 'Try to imagine what it would be like living in a society where there was no knowledge at all of history.'

The idea here is simply that history enables the society (and the individual within that society) to take its bearings, to place itself in relation to its own past, and in relation to other societies, and thus to establish a sense of its identity. *Identity* is one of the two key words here. The other one is *orientation*, which means 'finding our bearings': the study of history helps us to *orientate* ourselves. Thanks to our knowledge of history we find that instead of being totally adrift on an endless and featureless sea of time, we do have some idea of where we are, and of *who we are*.

The social importance of history is brought out by the way in which, even in everyday life, we are constantly coming up against history. In almost every conversation, even the most private, or, alternatively, even the most trivial, you will find references to history creeping in. Discussion of fashion will almost inevitably involve some reference to the *history* of fashion. Anyone who says that morals are going down the drain, is immediately making a historical point since he is comparing morals today with morals at some point in the past. (One must be careful here of course: the knowledge being drawn upon may simply be personal memory, which is not quite the same as history; but on the whole I think you will find it true that it is genuine, if hazy, historical knowledge which is brought in.) Certainly any discussion of politics will almost certainly involve a historical judgement. And if you look around you at houses, buildings, churches, immediately you are involved in some kind of historical contact with the past from which these buildings originated.

Even if we ignore all this – even if we look blindly at the buildings around us, and never indulge in serious general conversations – nonetheless, whether we like it or not, much of what happens to us in our own lives is governed by developments which took place in the past, or sometimes (and this is a rather subtle point) by what people *thought* happened in the past. For example, in Britain we live in a relatively free and tolerant society: this freedom and tolerance springs directly from certain historical circumstances. It may be, however, that we are also affected adversely by certain wrong decisions made by politicians who have misunderstood Britain's position as far as, say, the history of her imperial strength is concerned.

The point is that whatever way we turn we cannot escape from history, this time in all three senses of the word. But if history in all three senses has this importance, then clearly it is also important to further the scholarly study of history in as efficient a way as possible. If we are constantly encountering history, we should want it to be 'good' history rather than inadequate or 'bad' history.

Does this justification for the study of history seem rather elaborate to you? Quite possibly you have had in mind rather more straightforward reasons for studying history. Perhaps you would now like to pause and note down any such reasons.

EXERCISE

Note down any reasons which you believe to be valid, or which you have heard other people put forward, for the study of history.

SPECIMEN ANSWER

Here is my list of most of the points which are usually made. Probably you have not got nearly as many as this, and you may well have grouped some of the points in a rather different way.

1 History is enjoyable, just as is the study of painting or of music.

2 There is a 'poetic' appeal about history which attracts at least certain types of people to its study.

3 History is an intellectual exercise, in the same way as any other intellectual pursuit, such as mathematics, or philosophy. It thus provides a valuable 'training of the mind', and assists critical judgement and the systematic presentation of arguments.

4 History is a good form of 'humane' or 'liberal' education: it tells us about man in his various activities and environments and thus helps us to know and understand our fellow human beings.

5 History, being concerned with the totality of man's past experience, is central to all understanding of man and society.

6 History equips us to deal with the problems of the contemporary world.

7 History is part of man's continuing attempt to understand (and control) himself and his environment, physical and social; by contributing to our understanding and our control, it also contributes to our freedom as human beings.

8 Being fundamentally concerned with the study of evidence, history provides us with a specially valuable training in dealing with the deluge of conflicting evidence (in newspapers, on television etc.) which assaults us all the time in everyday life.

9 (To restate the justification I have already dealt with in full.) History is a social necessity.

10   History creates a disinterested curiosity, a way of escape from introspective selfhood.

11   History enables us to predict the future.

DISCUSSION

Obviously, some of these points overlap. Personally I would regard 5 as a restatement in more academic form (and therefore an extension and reinforcement) of my own basic point 9. But you might well regard 4, 5, 6 and 7 as saying rather the same thing in slightly different ways. Or, alternatively, 7 might be held to include at least two rather separate points within the one sentence. Equally, point 2 might be regarded as a special case of point 1; or one might (as I would) hold it to be part of point 9 (an individual expression of the argument that men *need* history); or it might be linked with point 10 (special commendation if you noted this one – it comes from the last page of *The Age of Humanism and Reformation* where Professor Dickens cites Samuel Johnson and Arnold Toynbee in support).

Since we are dealing with the different justifications different people tend to give for the study of history it is probably not worthwhile attempting a rigid categorization of what, in the end, is a pretty personal matter. But I would like you to reflect carefully on this list for a moment or two.

To make my own position clear: I would regard point 9, together with its main corollaries (as I see them), points 5 and 7, as the fundamental justification for the study of history. I would regard point 8 as an important practical subsidiary justification.

EXERCISE

Do any of the eleven justifications seem rather dubious to you?

SPECIMEN ANSWER AND DISCUSSION

I think we would have to rule number 11 out of court. So far the study of history certainly has not enabled us to predict the future, and most professional historians would argue that this is in no sense anyway the business of history. Point 6 might also be held to be rather strongly pitched. It is certainly part of my social necessity argument that history helps us to deal with the problems of the contemporary world, but it is scarcely true that history alone equips us to do this. History, one might say, would have to be taken in conjunction with a knowledge of the social sciences and, say, technology. Perhaps you may feel, too, that history (so far, anyway) is very far from enjoyable! Perhaps, too, you do not believe in the poetic appeal of history.

Anyway, as I say, these are fairly personal matters; but I do want you to reflect on them.

It is true that many famous historians, for example A. J. P. Taylor, argue that the only justification for the study of history, is the first one, that it is enjoyable. Yet I want to put a question to you here on this point.

EXERCISE

Even if historians themselves say that the basic justification for the study of history is purely its enjoyment, can you see how it could be argued that, despite what such historians say, nonetheless history does have a social utility?

Figure 1   Monumental nineteenth-century middle class housing, North Kensington: socially it has gone down in the world in the twentieth century.

Figure 2 · Twentieth-century middle class housing, Hendon: an attempt to create the rural atmosphere in the city.

Figure 3   View from hillside of Rooksmoor Mills, near Stroud, Gloucestershire. Although the buildings are late nineteenth century the former importance of the site is depicted by the number of seventeenth- and eighteenth-century clothiers' houses alongside (L. F. J. Walrond).

Figure 4   Coal mining in the Rhondda Valley, Glamorgan (Aerofilms Ltd).

Figure 5   Coventry Cathedral: twentieth-century cathedral, mediaeval ruins, and memories of the blitz of November 1940 (Tayler Bros, Coventry).

Figure 6   Free Trade Hall, Manchester. Built on the site of the 'Peterloo Massacre' to the glory of 'Free Trade'. Great civic hall and home of the Hallé Orchestra (Keith Gibson).

SPECIMEN ANSWER AND DISCUSSION

The argument would run something like this. Even if a man himself says that he does something simply because it is enjoyable, it may still be that the activity (enjoyable to him) is *useful*, or indeed (as I would argue) necessary to society as a whole. The position is in fact rather like that of the artist who says he paints simply because he likes painting and that he is not interested in whether society needs his painting or not: even though *he* says this, it may well be that there is a basic human desire for art which makes his paintings (*enjoyable* for him) *useful* for society. In other words, just because an individual historian justifies *his* study of history on the grounds that *he* enjoys it, that does not necessarily contradict the wider general justification that there is a social value in the study of history.

EXERCISE

Now just to see if you have grasped the various sorts of justifications that can be put forward for the study of history I am going to list a number of statements about history which imply or correspond to one of the justifications for history already given, and I want you to put the appropriate number (1-11) in the box beside the statement.

(a) Britain paid a terrible price for the ignorance of the facts and trends of European history shown by her leaders before the war.

(b) History is perhaps the greatest humanist medium of our time, educational and cultural.

(c) There exists in the human imagination an instinctive wish to break down the barriers of time and mortality and so to extend the limits of human consciousness beyond the span of a single life.

(d) History is the sextant and compass of states, which, tossed by wind and current, would be lost in confusion if they could not fix their position.

(e) The fundamental justification for historical study is its concern with the critical examination of sources.

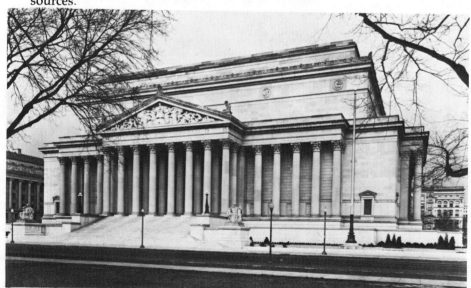

Figure 7 National Archives, Washington. Underneath the statues are inscribed 'What is Past is Prologue' and 'Study the Past'. High up around the walls are the following inscriptions: 'The glory and romance of our history are here preserved in the chronicles of those who conceived and builded the structure of our nation'; 'The ties that bind the lives of our people in one indissoluble union are perpetuated in the archives of our government and to their custody this building is dedicated'; 'This building holds in trust the records of our national life and symbolizes our faith in the permanency of our national institutions.' What do you think of these as justifications for the study of history? (Gift Collection in the National Archives).

SPECIMEN ANSWERS

(a) 6.   (c) 2 (or, perhaps, 10). (e) 8.

(b) 4.   (d) 9 (or its
                                     corollaries, 5 and 7).

DISCUSSION

These should be pretty straightforward, but if you do not understand my answers, go back and read this section again.

3 THE BASIC CONCERNS OF THE HISTORIAN

These basic concerns are:

(a) man in society;

(b) change through time;

(c) the particular and the unique.

3.1 MAN IN SOCIETY

We have got as far as defining the 'history' with which we are concerned in this course as 'the historian's attempt to reconstruct and interpret the past'. But the past goes back a long way! Unlike the geologist the historian is not concerned with the physical origins of the earth; nor is he concerned with the study of prehistoric monsters; even in the centuries with which he is concerned he does not pay direct attention to the movements of the stars or changes in the structure of the earth's surface – though he does become interested the moment any of these movements or changes impinge upon human activities.

And here we have a basic clue to the concern of the historian – apparent enough, really, from what we said about the justifications for the study of history: the historian is only interested when *man* comes on the scene. Just when exactly that was, of course, is a matter for biologists and anthropologists, rather than historians. A rather rigid distinction used to be made between 'pre-history' and 'history'. This distinction derived from the (correct) idea that since history (in the sense we are henceforward concerned with) is the historian's interpretation of the past, it can only begin to exist when the historian has reliable sources on which to base his interpretation. It was reinforced by the (dubious) idea that such sources must take the form of written records. In fact, as we shall see in the next unit, historians now call upon a much wider range of sources than mere written records, so that it is no longer worthwhile maintaining the rigid distinction between pre-history and history.

Most of our knowledge of the earliest human times is in fact due to the work of archaeologists and anthropologists. But archaeologists and anthropologists have also made extremely valuable contributions to the study of quite modern times. So again it is silly to make a rigid distinction between say, the periods of study appropriate to the archaeologist, and those appropriate to the historian.

Archaeologists have to possess deep professional skills to which the ordinary historian could not lay claim; yet, if we look at history in the very widest sense of the attempt to reconstruct the past, then archaeology (as many distinguished archaeologists have themselves said) is a form of historical study. It is not necessary to pursue this point further: all that has to be stressed is that, beyond the simple fact that history is concerned with the study of the past, it is concerned with the study of men in society.

In a way the last two words of this statement are unnecessary: men *do* live in societies. However it is best to keep these words in, since there has sometimes been an unfortunate tendency to write history as the exploits of individual figures, without reference to their social context. This is not to say that history should ignore the achievements of kings and generals, explorers and inventors. In one way or another such 'great men' have affected the development of hosts of lesser men and of whole societies and civilizations; they are therefore of great interest to the historian; but the historian must always have an eye on the wider implications: he should not study his 'great men' in, as it were, a vacuum.

3.2   CHANGE THROUGH TIME[1]

Man in society is also the concern of the various social sciences (anthropology, sociology, economics, political science and government, etc.) – hence the title of the Social Sciences Foundation Course in this university: *Making sense of society*.[2] Sociologists, political scientists, etc. are naturally concerned with the problems of social and political *change*; yet, in the last analysis, the characteristic which marks history out from these other disciplines is a specific concern with the element of change through time. Putting it very roughly, the social scientist looks for the common factors, the regular patterns, discernible in man's activities in society; the historian looks at the way societies differ from each other at different points in time, how, through time, societies *change* and *develop*.

We shall return to these issues when we discuss the question of whether history should itself be regarded as a social science (section 6, p. 44). Meantime what we are stressing is that history does in some sense *tell a story*: it must contain narrative, a sense of movement through time. Again, of course, we must not be too rigid about this: history requires explanation and analysis as well as narrative. A mere list of dates and events is a chronicle, not history: a writer of such a list is a chronicler or annalist, rather than in the fullest sense a historian. (Yet, while it is important that you should be able to distinguish mere chronicle from history remember that because of this basic concern with change through time, the historian often has, as a fundamental and difficult task, the establishment of just *exactly when* some events took place – we cannot *analyse* events till we know the exact order in which they took place.)

Sometimes the particular piece of work a historian sets himself will be exclusively concerned with analysis and explanation, and will not contain any explicit sense of change through time. But the historian will regard this piece of work as contributing to the wider view of history in which there will be a sense of change through time. For example one historian may devote his researches to a detailed study of what village life was like in England in the later thirteenth century: there will be analysis in depth, but little or no sense of movement through time. Another historian may similarly be occupied in a study of village life in the early fifteenth century. Before long a third historian will come along: putting these two studies together (no doubt along with other work of his own) to give a wider view, he will be able to bring out the *change* which has taken place between the late thirteenth century and the early fifteenth century.

3.3   THE PARTICULAR AND THE UNIQUE

The other point we have to make about history at this stage is that it must be concerned with what *did actually happen* to man in society in the past. In the examples just cited the historian will be concerned with what village life was actually like in the late thirteenth century and the early fifteenth century, rather than with making statements about village life in general. If he has studied enough different examples of village life in different centuries, the historian may well decide to offer some broad statements about village life in general: but he must start off with particular examples. And even if the historian has a perfectly legitimate interest in what he believes to be recurrent patterns in human activities, he must always be sensitive to the uniqueness of past ages and events. There may or may not be patterns, but particular circumstances never recur in exactly the same way. It is a basic function of the historian to illuminate human experience by highlighting differences. Great historical writing will always be

---

[1]Of course all change is 'through time' – that is, 'over a period of time' – but I mean relatively long periods of time – centuries not days, years not minutes.
[2]The Open University (1975) D101 *Making Sense of Society*, The Open University Press.

concerned with the meaningful interconnections and parallels between different events. But beware of historical writing which jumps over the uniqueness of past ages and past experiences in order to produce facile parallels and generalizations. It may be of interest to you to note that much of my own historical research has been concerned with developing a general model to explain the relationship between war and social change: but, as a historian, my starting point must always be particular wars, particular and unique examples of social change.

We shall return shortly to the question of general statements in history (section 6, p. 45), but for the moment we should note this difference of emphasis between the historian and, say, the sociologist.

The historian is not, *in the first instance*, concerned to make general statements about man in society: he is concerned with the actual, particular, unique, and different experiences which have befallen man in society in the past. Depending upon personal predilection he may *then* proceed to identify general patterns.

EXERCISE

Listed below are a number of passages, some of which illustrate what has just been said about history's concern with man in society, with change through time, and with particular, unique events in the past. Some, however, are not really examples of historical writing at all, but come from works of geology, sociology, biology, political science, etc. Others again, are not proper historical writing, being chronicles or annals. In the box provided, mark a tick (✔) for the passages which illustrate true historical writing, and a cross (X) for the others. In your notebooks write a short comment explaining each decision.

1   . . . the enquiry emphasizes political culture as a determinant of political behavior. It assumes that a fruitful way to study Labour's foreign policy troubles is to examine the values, beliefs, and symbols that party members share: hence the emphasis on socialist principles. But the reader must not be misled by this. Nowhere is it claimed that there has been a one-to-one correspondence between the principles and Labour's actual behavior – between theory and practice. After all, political culture is only one determinant of behavior; also important is the objective environment, what Karl Popper has called the 'logic of the situation', which can constrain the range of choice and even lead intended actions astray by producing unforeseen consequences. An inescapable problem of all sound policy making is to recognize the environmental constraints and to make the necessary adjustments to them. Obviously, were the enquiry to stress the cultural variables of Labour's behavior to the point of neglecting the environmental determinants, it would be lacking in realism, and so I have been at pains to take the latter into account.

2   The problem arises because there are different aspects or as I shall call them, *dimensions* of religion. Whether we include Marxism as a religion depends on which dimension we regard as crucial for our definition. It will therefore be useful to analyse these various dimensions.

The Ritual Dimension

If we were asked the use or purpose of such buildings as temples and churches, we would not be far wrong in saying that they are used for ritual or ceremonial purposes. Religion tends in part to express itself through such rituals: through worship, prayers, offerings, and the like. We call this the *ritual* dimension of religion. About this, some important comments need to be made.

3   The crucial importance here assigned to religious experience might encounter the following criticism. Surely, it will be said, the truth of religion is discovered through revelation. For instance, Christian revelation is to be found in the words of the Scripture, which are themselves guaranteed by God. Is not an analysis in terms of the experiential dimension untrue to the actual beliefs of Christians?

This objection is an important one, and a discussion of it will serve to clarify further what we mean by experience, doctrine, and mythology. The first point to make is that we are not here primarily concerned to say anything directly about the truth of religion. It may well be that such a profound and widespread phenomenon in human history and culture will strike as conveying truth. But this is a philosophical and doctrinal question we are not here called upon to decide. We must first describe the facts about man's religious experience scientifically. Using this approach we need only say this: the idea that God's revelation is to be located in the words of scripture is a doctrine believed by many people; the theory of revelation is part of the doctrinal dimension of Christianity.

4   In the next few years the process of change occurred rapidly in many parts of Germany. A number of princes threw off their allegiance to the Papacy, for political as well as religious reasons. Luther's teachings acquired considerable popularity among the masses. Monks were leaving the monasteries and marrying. Many of the older forms of ritual were discarded, Luther himself left his sanctuary, Wartburg, in 1522 when he learned that a former associate, Andreas Bodenstein of Karlstatt, who had assumed leadership of the German reform, was attempting radical changes and causing chaos and discontent. Luther restored order. In 1525, he married a former nun, Catherine Von Bora (1499–1552). In the same year his popularity declined considerably, because of his attitude towards the peasants.

5   Along the coast from Provence was Italy, splendid but politically chaotic. Its entire population was perhaps half that of France, but it was divided into a score of little states. The Venetian

republic, the most stable, had substantially more than a million inhabitants in its Italian territories. West of it was the duchy of Milan, with nearly a million people, but with less to boast of in government or in the arts. Florence, smaller still, under its Medici rulers, was the most brilliant centre of art and intellect in all Europe. Round these were crowded the duchy of Savoy, with its Alpine passes, the maritime republic of Genoa, the financial and commercial states of Siena and Lucca, and little fighting states ruled by *condottieri* who had troops for hire or, on occasion, for their own ambitious purposes. South of all these the papal dominion, the largest of all ecclesiastical principalities, ill governed and almost disintegrated among the nominally subordinate rulers of its towns, sprawled from sea to sea across the Apennines. The whole of the southern half of the peninsula belonged to the 'Kingdom', Naples, the only kingdom in Italy, sparsely peopled and numbering much less than a million inhabitants. Sicily belonged to the Spanish kingdom of Aragon, but had its own estates and administration.

6 In this survey of change during the later Middle Ages we have still to discuss a factor of paramount importance: the growth in the number, size, wealth, and sophistication of cities. No development so deeply modified feudal society, together with its religious and social attitudes. Throughout the twelfth and thirteenth centuries Kings and other rulers had readily chartered innumerable towns in return for money, yet no one can have realised the immensity of the changes this process was furthering. Throughout these same centuries urban growth had already been strongly stimulated by the development of sea-borne trade. The Near East had been opened up by the Crusades, the chief beneficiary of which proved to be Venice, the *entrepôt* between Asia and the overland route across the Alpine passes to central and northern Europe. Venetian and Genoese galleys, later joined by those of Spain, traded along the Atlantic coast. In Bruges and in London they met the ships of Hanseatic cities, which similarly dominated the Baltic and the north western ports. Meanwhile, as the plains of the east of Europe were colonised, a deep belt of walled towns replaced the primitive settlements of earlier days. The great mineral resources of Bohemia, Hungary, and Tyrol entered upon a phase of more intense exploitation. The old cities of Italy did not merely provide industrial experience and fine craftmanship. They also provided financial enterprise and method, together with a contemptuous rejection of the old ecclesiastical prohibitions against interest-taking. In the thirteenth century, banking houses had appeared in

Siena and Florence; they were soon lending large sums to the Kings of France and England. Venice and Florence stimulated their international trade by issuing gold coinages, and in due course their examples were followed not only in France, England, and Flanders, but also in Poland and Hungary. On the other hand, bills of exchange, which avoided the risky transport of volume, first developed in the Burgundian Fairs and were already multiplying rapidly around 1300. In European economic life the dominant and revolutionary process of the fourteenth century, and still more of the fifteenth, was the rise of a sophisticated capitalism.

7   The explanation that is often given and usually believed for the decline of Venetian society is that it was due to inbreeding of the ruling class. Any number of successful societies, tribal and civilised, however have been as inbred as the Venetian ruling class. Decline in all societies is connected, not with inbreeding or outbreeding as such, but with a switch from one to the other. Now, with a switch to inbreeding, such as happened in Venice, a second condition is indispensable for disaster. It is that the competition and selection which led to earlier success must be removed. This condition is, of course, the one which the Venetian ruling class, like any other, but with unusual success took steps to secure. For when it closed its gates in 1297 rejecting future recruitment of successful outsiders it established inbreeding and it eliminated internal competition in one step and, with the two exceptions we noticed, for ever.

8   *948* In this year king Edmund was stabbed to death, and Eadred, his brother, succeeded him; and straightaway he reduced all Northumbria to subjection: and the Scots swore him oaths and promised to do his will in all things.

949 In this year Anlaf Cuaran came to Northumbria.

952 In this year the Northumbrians drove out king Anlaf and accepted Eric, son of Harold, as their king.

954 In this year the Northumbrians drove out Eric, and Eadred succeeded to the Northumbrian kingdom.

955 In this year king Eadred passed away, and Eadwig, son of Edmund, succeeded to the kingdom.

956 In this year archbishop Wulfstan passed away.

959 In this year Eadwig passed away, and was succeeded by Edgar, his brother.

9   So there he stands, our vertical, hunting, weapon-toting, territorial, neotenous, brainy, Naked Ape, a primate by ancestry and a car-

nivore by adoption, ready to conquer the world. But he is a very new and experimental departure, and new models frequently have imperfections. For him the main troubles will stem from the fact that his culturally operated advances will race ahead of any further genetic ones. His genes will lag behind, and he will be constantly reminded that, for all his environment-moulding achievements, he is still at heart a very naked ape.

At this point we can leave his past behind us and see how we find him faring today. How does the modern naked ape behave? How does he tackle the age-old problems of feeding, fighting, mating, and rearing his young? How much has his computer of a brain been able to reorganise his mammalian urges? Perhaps he has had to make more concessions than he likes to admit. We shall see.

10 The term 'High Renaissance' has arisen chiefly by reference to the great painters and sculptors of the first three or four decades of the sixteenth century. For most educated observers this is first and foremost the age of Leonardo, Michelangelo, and Raphael, the age of Titian, Giorgione, and Correggio, while north of the Alps it is the age of Dürer and Holbein. When one compares the mature works of such artists with those of the *Quattrocento*, there can remain no doubt that their's is the high summer of art. Our individual tastes may perhaps incline to the early spring of the fourteenth century, or the late spring of Donatello's Florence, yet we could not possibly confuse the sequence of the seasons.

11 Some thousand million years ago, a star and the Sun passed by each other. The star was larger than the Sun, so that when they drew near the Sun suffered most from the mutual pull they exerted on each other owing to gravitation. Presently they became so close that their mutual pulls produced more than distortion, the gravitational pulls raised large tides as high as mountains on each star, but the tides on the Sun were the higher, because the Sun was the smaller star. As they approached still more closely the tide on the Sun grew so high that the wave reached up the Sun's sky and began to stream right out into space, towards the greater star.

SPECIMEN ANSWERS AND DISCUSSION

1 X

The material – Labour foreign policy since 1914 – is historical. But the *general*, rather *abstract* approach (for instance the interest in 'political culture' as a determinant of 'political behaviour' – whatever that means) rather than an interest in the *particular details* of Labour foreign policy and their *development through time* suggest that this passage comes from a work of political science rather than history.

2 ✓ or X

It's really very difficult to say on the basis of this short excerpt. We seem to have a rather abstract discussion of the nature of religion which scarcely fits the criteria laid down for historical writing. The passage in fact comes from the book you will be using a little later in the course *The Religious Experience of Mankind* by Ninian Smart. Though the sweep is wide, the approach in this book is basically historical. Obviously in studying the history of religion one has to give a good deal of attention to the nature of religion itself, just as in studying the history of science one has to give a good deal of attention to the nature of science itself. I cannot fault you if on the basis of this passage alone you say it is not history. Perhaps the best answer would be to say that it is history of religion, which I would regard as being a branch of history, though others might argue that this is a subject in its own right.

3   X

Here, in fact, we have the same author stating that his approach will be basically historical. However, this is clearly not history itself, but rather a statement of intended approach.

4   ✓

Here we clearly have a change through time, and a discussion of specific unique events related to man in society. Clearly this is a piece of historical writing. In fact it is from the quite definitely historical parts of Ninian Smart's book.

5 ✓

There is no sense of movement through time in this particular passage (and that may have led you astray), but its concern with the *exact* conditions of the Italian states in a *particular* period in the past (the fifteenth and sixteenth centuries) clearly identifies it as a work of history. It is from *Early Modern Europe* by G. N. Clark, and forms quite a nice piece of scene-setting for the study of the Renaissance which will link together the various examples in these three units.

6 ✓

Here we have important, specific changes through time relating to man in society. This is a very good piece of historical writing, and, of course, is from A. G. Dickens, *The Age of Humanism and Reformation* (p. 43).

7   X

Once more it's hard to say on such a short passage. The material has some similarity to that of 5 – the position of an Italian state (Venice) but this time in the thirteenth, not the fifteenth century. This could be by a historian with a strong interest (and why not?) in genetics. It is in fact by a *geneticist* (W. A. Darlington) with a strong interest in history. However you could, if you like, call this history, bringing out the wide range of interests covered by history.

8   X

This is mere *chronicle* not history. We get the list of events in time, but no analysis and explanation, no *interpretation* at all.

9   X

The writer here is concerned with the past (e.g. first line of second paragraph), but it should be pretty clear that this is a work of biology or zoology, not history. The book (*The Naked Ape* by Desmond Morris) is concerned with making *general* statements about the biology, psychology and social habits of man. Historians should be prepared to make use of the conclusions of books like this, but the book is itself not history: it is not concerned with the *particular*, *unique* activities of man, but with man in *general* – from, of course, the zoological point of view.

10 ✓

The content would seem to place this in the realm of art history, which involves particular skills of its own. In all respects it contains the criteria we look for in historical writing. Again, of course, it is from *The Age of Humanism and Reformation*.

11   X

This deals with the past all right. But not with man in society. It is astronomy not history.

4 THE SUBJECTIVE ELEMENT IN HISTORY

History is the historian's interpretation of the past. History, therefore, can never be completely objective ('objective' means 'unbiased' or 'strictly in accordance with the facts and uninfluenced by any personal feeling or prejudice'; the opposite of 'objective' is 'subjective').

This inevitable subjective quality in history is sometimes given as the reason for attacking history as an unsatisfactory subject. If history is merely personal interpretation, or, worse still, pure propaganda, then it does not merit serious study. However, to admit the personal, subjective element in history, is not to admit that history is no better than propaganda, or that it is simply a matter of opinion. Some such criticisms may, of course, be validly made of *bad* history. But most of the remainder of these three units will be devoted to explaining the very rigorous principles and methodology upon which *good* history is based.

Opinion has fluctuated over the extent to which even good history must in some degree be subjective. The first great pioneers of history as a discipline, in the nineteenth and early twentieth centuries (see section 5), believed that they were creating a completely objective 'scientific' history, based on the strict study of sources. They believed that if you searched the sources in a thoroughly 'scientific' way, eventually the 'facts would speak for themselves' – without any need for subjective interpretation. In the inter-war years of the twentieth century there was a swing in a different direction: the facts, it was decided, would never 'speak for themselves' without prompting from the individual historian.

Today few historians would accept either of these positions: it is generally held that although the subjective element can never be eradicated, the historian can, by the strict observance of certain principles, minimize the subjective element in his writing.

The subjective element which has received most attention is the one summed up in Professor E. H. Carr's famous phrase about history being a 'dialogue between present and past'. What is meant here is that each age tends to interpret the past in accordance with its own current prejudices and preoccupations. In the nineteenth century when British political institutions (and above all the British parliament) were the admiration of the world, there was a very strong emphasis on political and constitutional history. Victorian historians of mediaeval England were obsessed with a desire to see in mediaeval institutions something analogous to a nineteenth-century parliament – though historians are now agreed that the 'parliaments' of mediaeval England were vastly different from those of the nineteenth century.

In their studies of the eighteenth century, and particularly of the reign of George III, Victorian historians and their successors interpreted the political intrigues of the time in terms of Gladstonian liberals versus Disraelian conservatives – something no historian has dared to continue to do since the publication of Sir Lewis Namier's great works on politics in the late eighteenth century.

In the twentieth century, as we become more and more preoccupied with economic and social matters, as we begin to give more weight to the mass of the people instead of just to kings and political leaders, the emphasis in historical writing has moved towards economic and social developments.

This 'present and past' dialogue can never be completely suppressed. The historian can never entirely escape from the influences of the age and environment in which he lives. However to a degree this is true also of the sociologist, the geographer, and even of the natural scientist. In the past, no doubt, historians have too readily believed that they were being scientific and objective, and completely ignored this 'hidden influence' of their own environment and preoccupations. But now that historians recognize this 'hidden influence' they are much better prepared to take action against it.

EXERCISE

1   Recalling what has just been said about the inevitable subjective element in historical writing, comment in your notebook on these aims expressed by Lord Acton when in 1901 he was planning his *Cambridge Modern History* – a massive multi-volume collaborative enterprise between scholars of many lands (some of the names of these scholars are given at the end).

> Our scheme requires that nothing shall reveal the country, the religion, or the party to which the writers belong.
>
> It is essential not only on the ground that impartiality is the character of legitimate history, but because the work is carried on by men acting together for no other object than the increase of accurate knowledge.
>
> The disclosure of personal views would lead to such confusion that all unity of design would disappear . . .
>
> Contributors will understand that we are established, not under the Meridian of Greenwich, but in Long. 30°W.; that our Waterloo must be one that satisfies French and English, Germans and Dutch alike; that nobody can tell, without examining the list of authors, where the Bishop of Oxford laid down the pen, and whether Fairbairn or Gasquet, Liebermann or Harrison took it up.

2   Now turn to *The Age of Humanism and Reformation* and read the main long paragraph on page 8. Then read the middle paragraph on page 16. Do you detect any subjective influences in Professor Dickens's writing?

SPECIMEN ANSWERS

1   These aims seem a little impractical since in calling for complete impartiality, for a history which will satisfy all religions and all nationalities, the writer seems to be ignoring the inevitable subjective element in history.

2   Professor Dickens is of course too good a historian to allow his personal biases to distort his historical writing. However, the last sentence of the first paragraph I asked you to read suggests to me that Professor Dickens is conservative in political outlook – he appears to have little sympathy for 'modern democrats' and much sympathy for 'cultured Italian princes'; he also appears to blame the dictators of our own age on weak democracies. The second paragraph is perhaps more difficult, but here I noted the phrase in the middle about 'the desire to find social-economic explanations continued to our day unabated . . .' which suggests that Professor Dickens is strongly hostile to anything resembling Marxist explanations which tend to relate to everything to social-economic developments. A more moderate view might be that in some circumstances social-economic explanations are valid whereas, of course, in others they are not valid.

EXERCISE

1   Read this passage and see if criticisms of a different kind occur to you:

> The Second World War broke out in September 1939. It has been argued that Hitler's aggressive policies were the main cause of this, but it does have to be remembered that Germany felt many grievances over the conditions imposed on her at the end of the First World War. The British government has been blamed for failing to take a stronger line against Hitler, yet Chamberlain, the British Prime Minister, should perhaps be praised for striving at all times to preserve peace. The war lasted six years and soon involved all of the major world powers, including America and Japan. It has been argued that America was the only country to actually make a profit out of the war. On the other hand, had it not been for America, Germany might easily have triumphed.

2   In your notebooks write a short answer, defending history against the more extreme accusation that it is a highly subjective subject.

SPECIMEN ANSWERS

1   This passage goes to the opposite extreme of the ones in which we have detected subjective influences. The attempt has been made to be completely impartial and balance a statement inclining in one direction with another one balancing in the opposite direction. The result is an extremely boring piece of historical writing that brings out that if there is always a certain subjective quality in history, this is indeed no bad thing.

2   History does contain a subjective element. But this is true of other subjects, even science subjects, to a much greater degree than is sometimes believed: anything which brings in the human element, whether it be the setting up of a piece of scientific apparatus, or the carrying out of a social survey, must involve something of the human, personal element. What scientists and social scientists have to do is to try to cut down this subjective element to a minimum; and the same is true for history. Once the historian is *aware* of the kinds of subjective influences that will be operating upon him, he is that much better equipped to guard against them.

DISCUSSION

Obviously your answer will not coincide exactly with the one given above, and you may well have thought of other points not mentioned here. But the main points that you should have mastered are:

1   History probably is more subjective than some other subjects, but this is not undesirable since in the end history is the historian's *interpretation* of the past.

2   All disciplines do in fact have a slight subjective element in them. (Some of you will be in a position to note that mathematics as taught in the Foundation Course in Mathematics[1] at this university differs considerably from the mathematics you may have been taught elsewhere.)

3   Historians have become increasingly aware of the subjective influences derived from the preoccupations and prejudices of the particular era in which they happen to live; historians can thus be on their guard against these influences, even if they can never completely surmount them.

Perhaps there is a crucial difference between history and the physical sciences; perhaps history is, in a critical way, more subjective than science, while science is critically more objective than history. Rosalind Hursthouse takes up this point in Units 13–15, *Introduction to Philosophy*; I return to it briefly in section 6.

[1]The Open University (1971) M100 *Mathematics: A Foundation Course,* The Open University.

5 THE DEVELOPMENT OF THE MODERN DISCIPLINE OF HISTORY

I have talked of the emergence of history as a discipline in the early nineteenth century; and I have also said something of the change in views over the years about how far history can be objective. It is now time to give you a brief outline of the main developments in historical study since the nineteenth century. In general this particular section of the course is perhaps less important than most of the other ones. Certainly there is little value in your simply memorizing the names of a handful of famous historians. Inevitably in a short space it will only be possible to mention a few out of the thousands of historians who have been at work since the beginning of the nineteenth century. Since the names given here would not necessarily be the names accepted as the most significant by all historians, you should be careful not to take what is presented here as a complete history of history since the nineteenth century.

On the other hand any student of history, at anything beyond the most superficial level, ought to have some knowledge about the great pioneers of historical

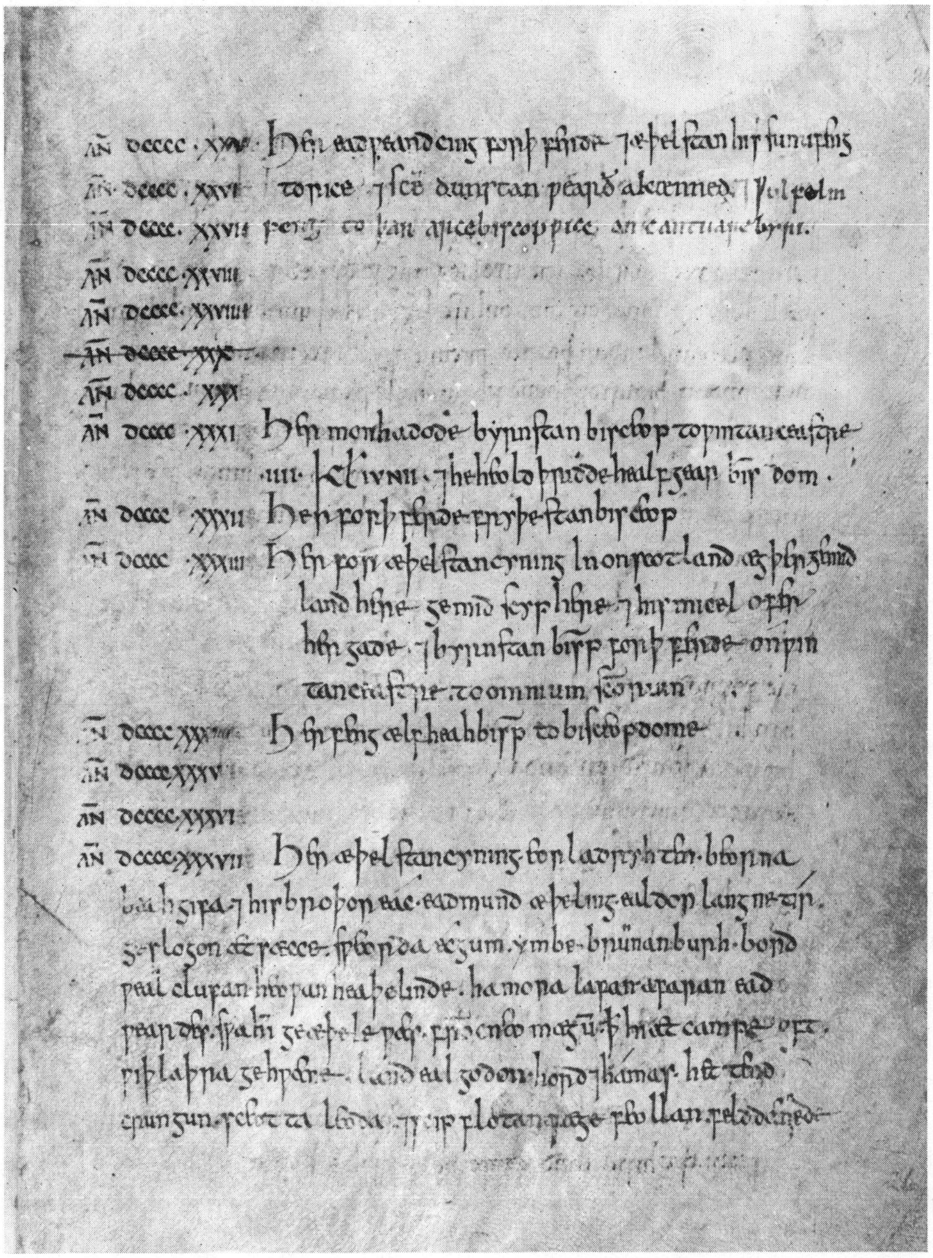

Figure 8   Excerpt from the Anglo-Saxon Chronicle (CCC, Ms 173, fol. 26r) (Master and Fellows of Corpus Christi College, Cambridge).

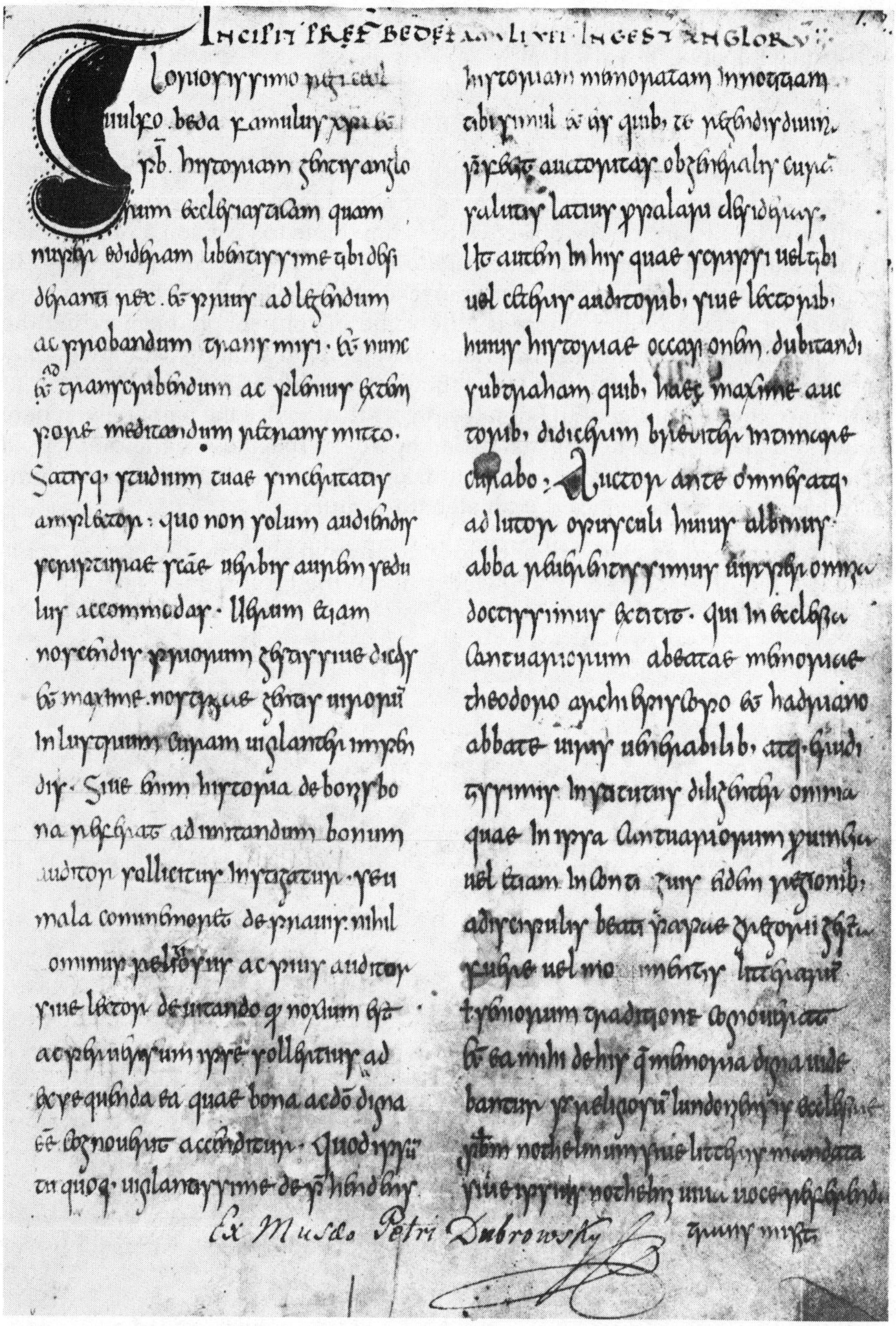

Figure 9 Bede manuscript: first page of Historia Ecclesiastica gentis Anglorum, *c. 731 (State M. E. Saltykov-Schredin Public Library, Leningrad).*

study. What you should get out of this section is a clear idea about the main movements in historical study which have permanently affected the way in which history is studied, and taught: positivism and Marxism are two outstanding examples of this kind of movement.

As we noted in section 1, historians of one sort or another have been at work from the beginnings of human society. And most people have vaguely heard of some of the more famous ones, such as Bede in the early Middle Ages, and Voltaire and Gibbon in the eighteenth century. As already stressed, it would be quite wrong to write off these historians as unscholarly and unworthy of attention. In terms of the broad second definition of history given in section 1 these men are great historians; nonetheless it is important that you should understand why history at the end of the eighteenth century cannot be regarded as a *discipline.*

34

Effectively there were three weaknesses in history as it existed at the end of the eighteenth century:

1   Although many scholars at various times had made brave efforts to base their work on genuine *primary sources* (the basic contemporary 'raw material', as distinct from histories written by other scholars – primary sources will be defined more precisely in our next unit), there was no systematic use of sources and there were no accepted methodological principles. Among some of the great eighteenth-century historians there was a tendency to rely upon secondhand accounts rather than upon primary sources. To be fair, one of the problems affecting pre-nineteenth-century historians was that, often, important collections of documents – for example documents belonging to kings or dukes or to the Papacy – were not open for inspection.

2   Eighteenth-century historians and most of their predecessors had very little real sense of the idea of change through time, of one age having particular and unique qualities of its own, different from those of another age. Both Gibbon and Voltaire had the habit of exercising their magnificent wit at the expense of earlier ages, criticizing the men of the middle ages for not coming up to the standards of civilization and behaviour expected of eighteenth-century high society. This is fundamentally an unhistorical attitude, failing to see, in a well-worn, but useful cliché, that 'times change'; that the men of the middle ages should be studied on their own terms, not treated as an assortment of curiosities. Only with a developed sense of the idea of movement and change in history; only with a full recognition that each age is different from its predecessors, and its successors, and yet is at the same time worthy of attention and understanding in its own right: only then could there be a genuine discipline of history.

3   Though there was some teaching of history in the various universities, it was not organized in any very systematic way: the main emphasis was on Greek and Roman history or on legal history. The chairs of modern history established at Oxford and Cambridge in the early eighteenth century were pretty exceptional, and their incumbents were essentially political favourites rather than genuine scholars.

The man who did more than any other to attack these weaknesses, it is widely agreed, was the Berlin historian, Leopold von Ranke; though credit in the matter of pioneering the systematic study of primary sources should also be given to his Danish-born contemporary in Berlin, Barthold Niebuhr. Niebuhr's most important period of activity lay between 1810 and his death in 1831. Ranke turned his attention to historical scholarship in the 1820s and continued to write and teach for most of the rest of the nineteenth century.

Taking Ranke as the representative and leader of the Berlin school, let us glance quickly at some of his more obvious achievements. First of all, he insisted that any piece of historical writing must be firmly based on the *primary sources,* and he made immense efforts to read as widely as he could in all the relevant archive collections, before writing any of his many books (though he was fortunate in that it was just at this time that many of the archives, which had been closed to historians for so long, were now thrown open, at least to such favoured historians as the ultra-conservative Ranke). In the preface to his first book, *History of the Latin and German Nations from 1494 to 1514,* Ranke made clear the fundamentals of his approach to history:

> The basis of the present work, the sources of its material, are memoirs, diaries, letters, diplomatic reports and original narratives of eye witnesses; other writings were used only if they were immediately derived from the above mentioned or seemed to equal them because of some original information.

More than this, Ranke explained, the book would include the full scholarly apparatus (references, footnotes, bibliography, etc. – discussed in Unit 5, section

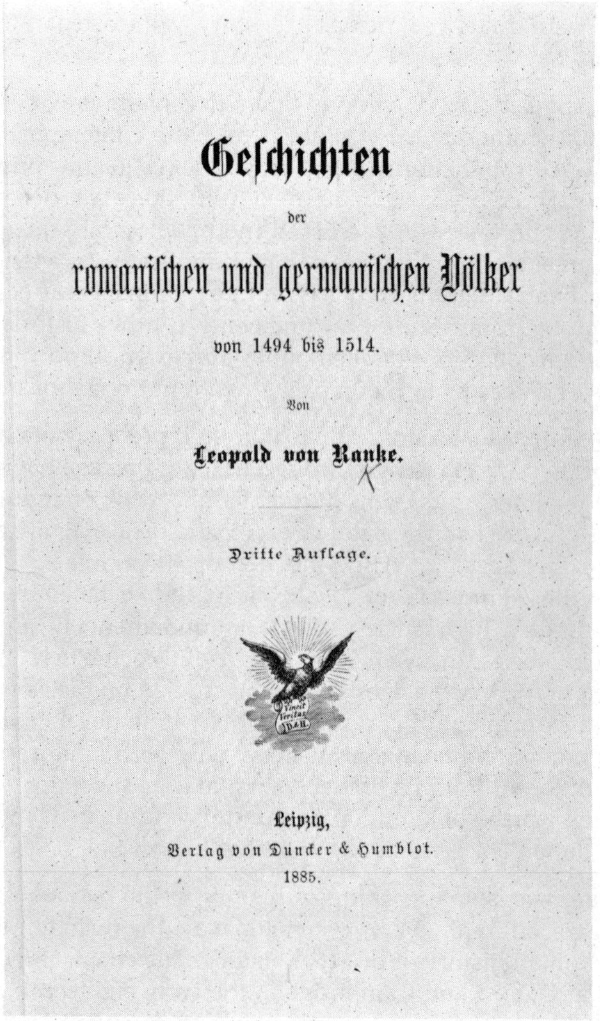
Geſchichten

der

romaniſchen und germaniſchen Völker

von 1494 bis 1514.

Von

Leopold von Ranke.

Dritte Auflage.

Leipzig,

Verlag von Duncker & Humblot.

1885.

Figure 10 Title page of Ranke's Geschichten der Romanischen und Germanischen Völker von 1494 bis 1514, *1885 (Reproduced by permission of the British Library Board).*

5): 'these sources will be identified on every page; a second volume, to be published concurrently, will present the method of investigation of the critical conclusions.'

Here we see, in brief, but clear words, the very essence of the new scholarly emphasis, not only on primary sources, but also on identifying these sources for the reader's benefit. And we also see Ranke's emphasis on 'method of investigation' and 'critical conclusions' – these words suggest, what Ranke certainly intended, that history was now presenting itself *as a science*.

It was in this same preface that Ranke made another important statement which set the key for the modern discipline of history which is, in the first place, based on primary sources, and, beyond that, concerned to understand the past on its own terms, from the inside, as it were, rather than as 'an assortment of curiosities':

> to history has been assigned the office of judging the past, of instructing the present for the benefit of future ages. To such high offices this work does not aspire: it wants only to show what actually happened.

This last phrase has often been quoted in mocking fashion; and undoubtedly Ranke was unduly optimistic in his estimate of how far study of the primary sources could yield an exact, objective, scientific account of 'what actually happened'. On the other hand this aim must be the *aim* of all scholarly history even if we admit that in the end subjective influences will never be completely overcome. It was Ranke's achievement, for all his defects, to set history firmly on this course.

Here, then, we see how Ranke attacked the first two of the weaknesses we list above. Many other individuals assisted in this task. In fact the entire Romantic Movement (the artistic, literary and intellectual movement – personified by such novelists as Sir Walter Scott – which strongly influenced European thought in the early nineteenth century) fostered a great interest in the past, involving both the attempt to see the past on its own terms, and the search for genuine sources dating from the past.

Ranke played a particularly important part in countering the third weakness in historical study, being responsible for developing the systematic teaching of the new discipline of history at the University of Berlin, particularly through his famous seminars in which he instructed advanced students in the technique of using primary source materials. In general other countries lagged behind Germany in instituting the systematic study and teaching of history. It is not really till the later part of the nineteenth century that history became established in the main universities (and therefore in the main schools) in the other Western countries. However, it can be said that by the end of the nineteenth century, history was firmly established as one of the most important subjects in all the leading universities. Almost everywhere 'history' meant *political history*, *diplomatic history* (foreign policy, the relations between different countries) or *constitutional history* (the study of organs of government, courts and parliaments).

Yet, while the particular approach to history pioneered by Ranke was making progress, a rather different approach to history was also developing in the middle part of the nineteenth century. With Ranke and his followers the emphasis was on the detailed accumulation of exact facts leading to a re-creation of the particular and unique events of the past. Influenced by the great scientific advances of the nineteenth century, several leading intellectual figures endeavoured to create a kind of history which would be 'scientific' in the completely different sense of presenting general laws analogous to the laws of the natural sciences.

The first great pioneer of this approach was August Comte (main period of activity, the 1830s), who is now widely regarded as the founder of modern sociology, but who left definite influences on historical study. Briefly Comte's idea was that man in society could be studied in just the same way as scientists

Figure 11   Auguste Comte, 1798–1857 (Maison d'Auguste Comte, Paris).

study the physical phenomena of the natural world; he hoped to discover definite 'laws' of historical and social behaviour. For example, Comte formulated his famous 'law of the three states' which stated that the history of all societies and all branches of experience must pass through three stages, which he called the Theological, the Metaphysical, and the Scientific. In the last analysis we would have to describe this approach as basically *unhistorical*, since, as already explained, the historian must start off from the particular and the unique; he must be more interested in what actually did happen than in abstract general laws about human and social behaviour.

But Comte's approach, which he called *positivism*, can be regarded as a valuable corrective to the studies of the Rankeans which were so concerned with unique events and exact detail, that at times they seem completely shapeless.

Even more important in developing an approach to history which postulated general laws and broad patterns is Karl Marx. Marx's writings are scattered over the period from the 1840s to the 1880s. Simplifying a little, it is, however, possible to present a brief summary of the main lines of this thought – the *Marxist*, or *materialist conception* of history (sometimes also called the *Marxist interpretation* or the *materialist interpretation*, or simply *Marxism* – though when the word Marxism is used this generally implies a political as well as a historical standpoint).

Figure 12   Karl Marx, 1818–1883 (Mansell Collection).

Marx first of all made a fundamental distinction between the basic economic structure of any society, determined by the conditions under which wealth is produced in that society, and the 'super-structure' by which he meant the laws, institutions, ideas, literature, art, etc.

Secondly, he argued that history (in our very first sense of the word, history meaning the past) has unfolded through a series of stages: *Asiatic, antique, feudal,* and *modern bourgeois* – each of these stages being determined by the prevailing conditions under which wealth is produced (e.g. in the feudal stage wealth is derived from ownership of land, in the bourgeois period it is derived from ownership of factories, etc.).

Thirdly, the motive force for this development from stage to stage is provided by the 'class struggle', classes themselves being determined by the relationship of particular groups to the specific conditions under which wealth is produced. The bourgeoisie (or middle class), for example, are the class who own the means of production in modern capitalist industrial society. Previously they led the class struggle against the dominant group in the feudal stage, the aristocracy. Now (in the *modern bourgeois*, or *capitalist* period) they find themselves engaged in a struggle with the class below, the proletariat, or working class.

Fourthly, Marx argued that at the end of each stage a point is reached where new productive forces come into conflict with existing class relations, and then there begins, in Marx's own words an 'epoch of social revolution'. There was 'social revolution' when feudal society gave way to capitalism; and there will be further 'social revolution' when capitalism begins to collapse.

Behind this view of the unfolding of history lies the notion of the 'dialectic', which Marx took over from the German philosopher Hegel (more about him later) – though Marx 'stood Hegel on his head' in applying the dialectic to material developments, not ideas. The basic notion is that each historical stage contains within it a contradiction which will lead on to the creation of the new stage – put crudely the notion of the dialectic means the confrontation between the two forces, the original historical stage, and the contradiction within it.

In a real sense the Marxist scheme is unhistorical in so far as it puts this grand pattern *before* exact study of the actual events of history. It runs the danger of looking at the past, *not* on its own terms, *not* from the inside, but simply as convenient material to illustrate the unfolding Marxist theory. However, if Marxism (or the Materialist conception of history – this alternative name arises from the emphasis placed on the 'economic structure' as determining ideas, politics, etc., rather than ideas being the determining element as the opposing school – the 'Idealists' – would say) is treated in an intelligent, sceptical way, it can be a very useful tool in the study of history. The fact is that when Marx was not engaged in political writing (and it must be remembered that he was basically a political thinker) his own approach to history was both thorough and imaginative. The most banal utterances have been perpetrated by minor followers of Marx; on the other hand some of the best history in the twentieth century has been written by imaginative, sceptical, followers of Marx, about whose devotion to hard, scholarly research there can be no reservations.

From the point of view of the development of historical study, Marx is important for:

1   stressing the importance of economic history, and

2   pointing a line towards a kind of 'total history', that is to say a history in which stress is laid on the inter-relationship between art, ideas, politics and economics;

3   one might perhaps also give him (along with Comte and others) credit for trying to create a kind of history which is a study of society, in the way in which modern social scientists understand the phrase, rather than just a detailed, shapeless picture of one thing happening after another.

In the twentieth century, three of the most significant developments in historical study have been (note: not all historians would necessarily agree with this section):

1 The development of an interest in economic history as a sort of specialist 'sub-history' analogous to the 'sub-histories' which the followers of Ranke developed in the nineteenth century; that is, constitutional history, and diplomatic history.

2 The subsequent attempt to restore the unity of history (which seemed in danger of fragmenting into too many 'sub-histories'), through the concept of 'total history'; a history stressing the inter-relations between all aspects of man's past activities. The most important pioneers of this approach are two French historians whose work began just before the First World War, and who directly influenced historical study until after the Second World War: Lucien Febvre and Marc Bloch.

3 The willingness to apply new methods and techniques to historical study, largely borrowed from the social sciences (including archaeology), but also from the natural sciences. (If you are interested, you can follow up these matters in chapters 2 and 3 of *The Nature of History*.)

This third development is tied up very closely with an interest which all writers in the twentieth century (novelists and poets as well as historians) have had in psychology, thanks largely to the epoch-making discoveries of the great Austrian psychologist, Sigmund Freud (his first studies were published at the beginning of the century, but only became widely known after the First World War).

4 A fourth characteristic of historical study in the twentieth century, therefore, has been an awareness, implicit or explicit, of the sub-conscious and irrational motives which lie behind human and social behaviour; and, in particular, of the influence of 'patterns of behaviour' which, unconsciously, influence the activities of men in groups.

As far as British historians are concerned, the greatest twentieth-century figure to date is probably Sir Lewis Namier. (Namier's first great studies of eighteenth-century politics were published in the late twenties and early thirties, but he reached his period of maximum influence only in the decade or so following the Second World War. He died in 1960.) His fame rests partly on his further development of the painstaking, 'scientific' techniques of Ranke (he built up his picture of politics by the 'multiple-biography' technique – hundreds of detailed biographies of individual politicians); but he is also distinguished by his distrust of high-flown theorizing about human motivation: he played down the influence of fine-sounding ideas on human actions, believing that such ideas usually conceal more basic motives (put at its crudest – and Namier was never crude – men go into politics for what they can get out of it, not to further abstract ideals). Above all Namier looked at the 'structure' (that is the 'pattern of behaviour' mentioned in the previous paragraph) of political activity.

In our own time historians have continued to practise all kinds and varieties of historical study. It would be quite wrong to try to pin down historical study today by any one characteristic. But it might reasonably be said that the best historians of today are those who, on the one hand, have some kind of concept of the *totality of history* (even if their own researches are necessarily confined to a fairly narrow field), and who, on the other hand, show a willingness to employ the *widest possible range of techniques* in their research.

EXERCISE

Some of the statements below form reasonably adequate summaries of important aspects of the development of the modern discipline of history; others are false. Show that you can distinguish between the reasonable statements and the nonsensical ones by placing a tick in the box beside the accurate ones, and a cross against the inaccurate ones.

1   Marx was the true pioneer of the modern discipline of history.

2   Both Ranke and Comte claimed to bring science to the study of history, though in rather different ways.

3   Bloch and Febvre tried to prevent history from breaking up into a series of separate specializations.

4   Sir Lewis Namier was one of the giants of nineteenth-century historical writing.

5   Before Ranke there was no systematic university-level teaching of history.

Das Kapital.

Kritik der politischen Oekonomie.

Von

Karl Marx.

Erster Band.

Buch I: Der Produktionsprocess des Kapitals.

Das Recht der Uebersetzung wird vorbehalten.

Hamburg

Verlag von Otto Meissner.

1867.

New-York: L. W. Schmidt. 24 Barclay-Street.

Figure 13   Title page of Marx Das Kapital, *1867 (Reproduced by permission of the British Library Board).*

ANSWERS AND DISCUSSION

1 X

Marx pioneered many things, but not this. If you got this wrong re-read the paragraphs about Ranke for his claim to be regarded as the pioneer of the modern discipline of history.

2 ✓

Ranke meant 'science' in the sense of painstaking accumulation of evidence; Comte meant it in the sense of formulating general laws.

3 ✓

If you got this wrong re-read what I have said about twentieth-century developments, and also what is said about Bloch and Febvre in *The Nature of History* pp. 72–7.

4 X

Sir Lewis Namier was one of the giants of *twentieth-century* historical writing.

5 ✓

If you disagreed re-read what I have said about the three weaknesses in history as it existed at the end of the eighteenth century.

Figure 14   Leopold Ranke, painting by von Schraeder (Mansell Collection).

Figure 15   Sir Lewis Namier, 1888–1960 (Radio Times Hulton Picture Library).

6 HISTORY AS SCIENCE, HISTORY AS ART, HISTORY AS ART AND SCIENCE

We have seen that both Ranke and Comte wished history to be approached scientifically. But although their attitude in part sprang from the same general faith which people of the nineteenth century had in the possibilities of science, in practice they meant rather different things. Ranke meant painstaking, careful, disciplined study of the evidence. Comte meant the attempt to formulate for human society general laws analogous to the laws which one finds in the natural sciences.

Occasionally today, historians still debate with themselves whether history is or is not a science. Clearly, as with so many such debates, much turns on questions of definition. If science is defined, as many European intellectuals define it, simply as 'an organized and systematic body of knowledge', then history, in our third sense of history as a discipline, is also a science. However, if we have in mind the examples of physics, chemistry, biology and so on, obviously there are differences between history and these subjects, though it may sometimes be difficult to pin down precisely what these differences are.

What I propose to do here is: first, to list some of the ways in which history can be said, in some sense, to be a science; and some of the arguments which suggest that history does in fact have much in common with physics, chemistry, etc. After that we shall look at the arguments often advanced to show either that history is *not* a science, as we commonly understand this word, or that history is not *just* a science.

First, the ways in which history is similar to the natural sciences: and the first of these is that the historian, as I hope to demonstrate in this three-week introduction to history, does have a definite methodology, a definite way of testing evidence and evaluating facts. In that sense history is a science.

Establishing 'facts' – in history and in the natural sciences – can be a difficult and exciting task; but in the end what is really interesting is the *relationship* between facts. In the nineteenth century scientists used to talk more confidently about *scientific laws* than they do today – for a scientific law is really a hypothesis or theory which seeks to explain the relationship between different facts: it is the simplest explanation of a series of facts consonant with all known facts and tested by experiment. At this level scientists today deal in *probabilities* rather than absolute certainties. One should therefore be careful about separating history from science simply on the (mistaken) grounds that science deals in terms of absolute provable certainties while history usually does not. (Note: I am deliberately phrasing this discussion in non-technical language, and I am not concerned with the scientific and philosophical arguments over 'probability theory'. Even so my colleague Oswald Hanfling tells me this paragraph is much too simple and sweeping. I am leaving it to him and Rosalind Hursthouse to sort things out later in the course. As far as I can make out, they don't in fact agree with each other in this history science discussion.)

Thirdly, although we have agreed that Comte's would-be scientific approach is unhistorical, this does not mean that historians are precluded for all time from presenting, if not general laws, certainly general formulations – perhaps about certain common features of revolutions, or about the processes of industrialization, or some other general theme of this sort. Not all sciences, on the other hand are completely governed by general laws; and certainly scientists usually proceed on the basis – once they have studied the 'evidence', that is, the results of their experiments – of formulating certain hypotheses which are subsequently confirmed or abandoned. This procedure (studying the data, formulating a hypothesis, then testing it) is not altogether different from that of the historian.

44

What these three arguments amount to is a statement that the lines between history and the natural sciences are by no means rigidly drawn, and that if one cares to define science simply as an 'organized body of knowledge', then history can be regarded as a science.

However, it is probably more interesting to study the ways in which history definitely does differ from most of the natural sciences. First of all the scientist in most cases has the power to conduct a controlled experiment as often as he likes till he has drawn all the conclusions he wishes to from it. The historian cannot conduct a controlled experiment; and he certainly cannot call upon a repeat performance from the past. In middle-range activities, then (that is, stopping rather short of offering theories about whether the universe is expanding or contracting, or new interpretations of relativity) scientists can usually offer a more definite *proof* than historians operating in the same range. The scientist's probabilities, if you like, are *more probable*. (The philosopher of science would probably prefer to say 'a different kind of probable', but that need not concern us meantime.)

Secondly, we have agreed that somewhere in historical study there must be a definite element of the subjective. It has already been argued (in section 4) that the scientist is never absolutely and completely objective: the man who assembles the apparatus for a particular controlled experiment in effect himself becomes a part of the experiment. Scientific observation, even if it amounts to no more than reading figures off a dial, is still *human* observation. Nonetheless it would be stupid to deny that the controlled scientific experiment depends appreciably less on the human element than does historical study.

Thirdly, whatever general formulations the historian may resort to from time to time, his basic objective is not usually the establishment of general 'laws'; indeed, as we have seen, the historian has a special interest in individual unique events and persons. For most scientists, on the other hand, the greatest triumph is the formulation of a new general law embracing a series of more limited laws. However much historians may generalize and hypothesize, there is, in the end, no equivalent in historical study to, say, the laws of thermodynamics or the special theory of relativity.

Fourthly, following from this, it is often said that science has the power, and aim, of prediction, while history has not. This can be allowed to stand in the sense that it is not the function of the historian (as historian) to predict the future (his concern, *as a historian*, is with the *past*; he may as a historically-trained citizen endeavour to predict the future). Actually the historian does get involved in a kind of prediction (sometimes called *retrodiction*) when he tries to work out what *might have happened in the past*. However this is a rather subtle point which you need not bother about too much meantime (if you are interested in taking it further, see *The Nature of History*, p. 100).

A fifth, and rather important distinction between history and the natural sciences is an extension of the point about history necessarily containing an important subjective element: there are times when the historian simply cannot avoid making value judgements of a type not encountered in the natural sciences. Ranke, as we saw wanted a history which did not 'judge the past'. Now that is a very praiseworthy aim: the historian whose main stock-in-trade is handing out good or bad marks to people and events in the past is a very bad historian, for the essence of the historical attitude is *understanding* the past, not *judging* it. Yet we saw (section 4, exercise p. 31) the disastrous results when the historian tries to be completely neutral. In fact the historian cannot avoid using words like 'massacre', 'faction', 'ambitious' and so on, all of which imply some kind of judgement. Furthermore in the mere selection of his facts, the historian is involved in judgement of a sort. Professor Knowles has written: 'The historian is not a judge, still less a hanging judge.' This is well said, and well worth remembering. But nonetheless the historian sometimes must be involved in making value judgements: this does distinguish him from the scientist.

One simple way of cutting through the problem would be to say, sixthly, that the real difference between history and the sciences lies in the *material studied*. History is concerned with the activities of man, the sciences with the phenomena of the physical universe (including, of course, animate objects such as flowers and animals, which, in turn, include man himself considered as *animal*). It could be said that all the other differences between history and the sciences spring from this basic difference; and some writers would argue that this is the most important one to concentrate on. Unhappily it does not settle the more complicated problem of history and the *social* sciences.

A seventh argument sometimes advanced is that while the sciences have *use*, history has none. By use is meant the production of television sets, antibiotics, jumbo jets and nuclear bombs. Two points have to be made here: first, if the social necessity of history is accepted, then history does have use; second, it is not in fact true that the activities of scientists are directly geared to use – the 'useful' products mentioned above are the work of applied scientists and technologists, they result only indirectly from the work of pure scientists.

Finally let us add an eighth argument which will be developed more fully in Unit 5: if the historian's activities do have value for society then they must be *communicated* to society. It is not usually considered a basic part of the scientist's duty to write up his results in a form understandable to other members of society; indeed his work may best be summed up in a few pages of equations. But historians, as a group, have failed if they do not from time to time produce clear, readable books.

The question of communicating, of writing clear, readable books takes us out of the world of the sciences back into the world of literature, the world of the arts. But before developing the question of history *as art* (instead of, or in addition to, history *as science*) we must look at the difficult matter of history's relationship with the social sciences.

Again this is in large measure a matter of definition, and, indeed of convenience. If faculty lines have to be drawn somewhere, should history line up with economics, sociology and political science (that is with the social sciences); or, as has traditionally been the case, with literature, philosophy and languages (that is, with the humanities, or arts)? The trouble is that history is, in a very real sense, a central subject: it has close relations with economics and politics on the one side, but equally close ones with philosophy and literature on the other.

Certainly, the sixth argument listed above for distinguishing history from the natural sciences (the material studied) does not apply in the case of the social sciences, which with the partial exception of geography, are no more concerned with the physical universe than is history itself. From out of the other arguments given above, it is however, possible to single out four which might be used to justify history's inclusion along with the arts, rather than with the social sciences: these are the first (the lack of controlled experiments and proof), third (the lack of hypotheses and general laws), fifth (the inevitability of value judgements), and eighth (the need for communication).

Controlled experiments and proof

Social scientists, unlike historians, do conduct 'experiments' in the form, principally of opinion samples, or studies of the reactions of controlled groups of human beings to certain stimuli. Much modern economic theory is presented in the form of mathematical equations. When it comes to a real human situation the theory may not in fact work, but at least in mathematical terms it is *provable* in a way that no historian's hypothesis is *provable*.

Hypotheses and general laws

The historian, we have seen, may present general formulations; but his first interest is in the particular and the unique. Social scientists, though they have not yet produced anything quite like the general laws of the natural scientist, are essentially orientated towards the universal, towards constructing abstract models representing general truths, rather than towards the detailed recreation of unique events.

Value judgements

Inevitably the subjective will intrude further into the work of the social scientist than it does into the work of the natural scientist; but through his greater use of controlled experiments and his greater resort to abstract models, the social scientist can avoid the constant entanglement with value judgements which besets the historian (or at least he thinks he can – there's a good deal of debate about this!)

Communication

Like the natural scientist, the social scientist does not have that direct involvement with a wide audience which is the direct consequence of the social function of history. The great historians are at least readable; many social scientists seem to derive a special pride from being totally unreadable – technical terms easily degenerate into jargon, and statistical methods are not easily converted into polished prose. (My colleague Christopher Harvie believes I overstate the differences between history and social science. Of course there are highly readable social scientists and highly unreadable historians. Furthermore 'pop sociology' has recently become a major growth industry. Nonetheless I would maintain that a quick comparison of any leading social science journal with any leading historical journal will confirm my point.)

With communication we turn back to the question of history as art. If we decide to agree, as many historians in the past, and today, have agreed, that history is both 'art *and* science' – that is, a *science* in the method and manner in which it studies the evidence and ascertains the facts, and an *art* in the way it communicates these discoveries – then the science must dominate the art, rather than vice versa. You have probably come across pieces of history which are brilliantly written, full of vivid rhetoric and elegant metaphors; but if the historical content is rubbish, then no amount of fine style will make them into good history – though provided they have some kind of content they may be excellent as examples of literary *art*.

Creative imagination is required in the highest flights of scientific theory; but on the whole the arts are distinguished from the sciences by the degree to which they call upon imagination and *intuition*. History which is all, or largely, intuition and no fact would be very bad history. But in the best historical writing there is a creative, intuitive element, well described by the distinguished historian, Richard Pares (you can check up on him in *The Nature of History*, pp. 146, 91) when he defined history as 'a series of bright ideas'.

What Professor Pares had in mind is that the work of the greatest historians is characterized by the gift of making brief, vivid pronouncements, which, though not provable in the way that a scientific formula might be provable, nonetheless seem absolutely right in the context of the entire interpretation which the historian is unfolding, and which somehow illuminate a whole historical problem. A splendid example occurs in the passage from A. G. Dickens I quoted earlier where he refers to the high Renaissance as a 'summer', as compared with the 'spring' of the earlier Renaissance. As you read through *The Age of Humanism and Reformation* look out for these 'bright ideas'.

EXERCISE

Read and compare the four passages given below. In the first column mark an *A* against the passage which seems to best exemplify history as *science*; in the second column mark a *B* against the passage which best exemplifies history as *art*; in the third column mark a *C* against the passage which strikes you as best as *history*. (It is quite possible that you might want to put two or even three of these letters against the same passage.)

1   The purpose of the four preceding chapters has been to argue that these other factors were numerous. The process of growth is complex, and any attempt to explain an industrial revolution in terms of a single prime mover is bound to be misleading. Inevitably a wide range of factors is involved, and each of these factors has its own chronology. Thus, the chronology of an industrial revolution is the sum of a large number of contributory chronologies. Since very few of the component variables can be stated in quantitative terms, the explanatory model cannot, inevitably, be assembled with anything approaching the degree or precision required by present-day theorists of economic growth. Nonetheless these manifold changes did occur in the eighteenth century, and the fusion of the many separate movements in the right order transformed the economy and society. For ease of analysis some of the component changes have been abstracted from the general body of social and economic development and examined separately in the previous chapters. Now it is time to reassemble the model, piece by piece, and, if possible, in the right order.

2   In the early-medieval world[1] two principal traditions of thought about the artist had rather uneasily co-existed. The first, which could be called loosely the Ecclesiastical-Roman Imperial tradition, saw him as an artisan whose function was to express the truths of religion at the behest and under the guidance of the ecclesiastic. So, in the second council of Nicaea of 787, where the Empress Irene struck at the iconoclastic heresy, it was decreed that:

> the form of images is not the invention of painters but is based on the traditions and tried legislation of the catholic church. And the composition and this tradition are not things which concern the painter. To him is entrusted

[1]For which see: F. Bologna, ' "Operis causa non fervor devotionis". Spunti di critica d'arte medioevale', *Paragone – Arte*, xii, no. 137, 1961, pp. 3–18; Johannes Jahn, 'Die Stellung des Künstlers im Mittelalter', *Festgabe für Friedrich Bülow*, ed. O. Stammer and K. C. Thalheim, Berlin, 1966, pp. 151–68; George Henderson, *Gothic* Harmondsworth, 1967, ch. i, 'The Gothic artist'.

only their execution. Rather do they depend on the order and disposition of the holy fathers.[2]

At the same time the role of the artist was further diminished by the long-remembered teaching of Gregory the Great. In two letters written at the end of the sixth century he had declared that: 'Paintings should be employed in churches for this reason, that those who are ignorant of letters, may, on seeing them, read on walls what they are not able to acquire from books.'[3] These words, frequently cited in the centuries which followed, did indeed give a valuable sanction to the employment of the artist by the church but they carried with them the implication that art itself was an activity particularly appropriate for the understanding of the uneducated and for the minds of the illiterate.

[2]*Sacrorum conciliorum nova et amplimissima collectio*, ed. J. D. Mansi, xiii, Florence, 1767, col. 672.
[3]Gregory I, *Registrum Epistolarum*, MGH. Ep., ii, pp. 195, 269–72.

3 Dante tells us that he saw, in Malebolge, a strange encounter between a human form and a serpent. The enemies, after cruel wounds inflicted, stood for a time glaring on each other. A great cloud surrounded them, and then a wonderful metamorphosis began. Each creature was transfigured into the likeness of its antagonist. The serpent's tail divided itself into two legs; the man's legs intertwined themselves into a tail. The body of the serpent put forth arms; the arms of the man shrank into his body. At length the serpent stood up a man and spake; the man sank down a serpent, and glided hissing away. Something like this was the transformation which, during the reign of George the First, befell the two English parties. Each gradually took the shape and colour of its foe, till at length the Tory rose up erect the zealot of freedom, and the Whig crawled and licked the dust at the feet of power.

4 One of the clearest differences between the seventeenth century and the twentieth is that nowadays government is conducted on the basis of statistics, but then there were scarcely any statistics to be had, and such as existed were very little used. Sir Robert Walpole, who was born in that century, said that in the British House of Commons a man could do more with figures of arithmetic than with figures of rhetoric. That may well have been the temper of the British politician even before his time; but if it was so, the material for gratifying it was very meagre. It was only towards the end of the seventeenth century that useful statistics began to be compiled and published in the more bustling countries.

SPECIMEN ANSWERS

Passage 1

Passage 2

Passage 3

Passage 4

A		
	B	*C*

DISCUSSION

There are two possible *A*s depending on which of the two meanings of scientific you have in mind.

Passage 1 leans towards science in the sense of seeking general laws, or at least abstract models. Passage 2 is scientific in the Rankean sense of building up a picture out of painstaking detailed research. You may, however, feel (if that is the way you prefer to regard 'science') that the most genuinely scientific is Passage 4, because of its simplicity and clarity.

Passages 1 and 2, however strong their other merits, are not very elegantly written, and so can scarcely be rated highly as art. Passage 3 is actually an excerpt from Macaulay's essay on 'Chatham' (for Macaulay see *The Nature of History*, pp. 43–5). If you like this sort of thing you might well give it top rating as art; many people would. Personally I prefer passage 4, which is from one of Sir George Clark's books, *The Seventeenth Century*: this is clear and elegant, and contains one basic and highly illuminating point (a 'bright idea' in fact) about the difference between the seventeenth and the twentieth centuries. (Note: it is not being argued here that the Macaulay passage is empty or meaningless – it would scarcely be art if it were. Nor is it being argued that all fine style must be of the Macaulay type.)

For me the real strength of this passage (4) is that it is good *as history*. The Macaulay certainly, is too fanciful to be good, reliable history. Passage 2, though competent, is a bit pedestrian. Passage 1 is interesting for its attempt to bring a 'social science' approach to historical study; perhaps we would regard it, as history, as runner-up to Passage 4.

If this discussion does not make sense to you, you must go back and again read carefully through the whole of section 6.

Unit 3 ends here. If you are ahead of time, get on with reading the set book.

UNIT 4 PRIMARY SOURCES
CONTENTS

OBJECTIVES OF EACH SECTION

Section 1 Historical Research

You should understand what the scholar means by 'research'. You should also understand the crucial distinction between *primary* sources, the basic contemporary raw material of history, and *secondary* sources, interpretations written later by historians.

Section 2 The Variety of Primary Sources

You should appreciate the variety and range of primary sources, which include archaeological remains, aerial photographs, archive film, etc., as well as the more obvious written sources.

Section 3 Witting and Unwitting Testimony

You should understand the fundamental distinction between the *witting testimony* of a primary source – the information which the original writer or creator of the source deliberately intended to convey to his own contemporaries – and the *unwitting* testimony – the information which the historian extracts from the source (about attitudes, assumptions, etc) which was in no way intended by the original writer.

Section 4 Criticism and Evaluation of Primary Sources

In a basic and elementary way you should be aware of the methods and techniques which the historian brings to bear on his primary sources.

Section 5 Literature and Art as Primary Sources

You should appreciate the special value and the special dangers of this type of source.

Section 6 The Imperfect and Fragmentary Nature of Historical Sources

This is one of the most important points to appreciate in reading *Introduction to History*. You should understand that the sources upon which the historian is dependent are extremely fragmentary and imperfect, and often very difficult to draw any clear, positive conclusions from at all.

Section 7 Communication

You should appreciate that apart from *research* the historian must be concerned with communicating his findings.

1 HISTORICAL RESEARCH

'Research' is a word you will meet quite frequently these days. Often at the end of a television programme, in addition to the credits for cameraman, producer, etc., you will see a little credit saying 'research by . . .'. What is meant here is that the basic material upon which the programme was based, as distinct from the organization and presentation of the programme, has been *discovered* by this 'researcher', who has consulted various books, sought information by personal interview, and so on.

This does give a slight clue to the meaning of research as used by scholarly historians. The slight clue is that research does involve *discovering* the basic material upon which a book, a thesis, an article, or even a television programme is based. There is no great harm in using the word 'research' in the loose way of the television programme-maker; and in fact you may, when you, as a student, are writing an essay, be tempted to say, when you visit your local library, that you are doing the 'research' for your essay.

But for the academic historian 'research' has a rather stricter meaning; and if you yourself are to be able to distinguish between good history and bad history, you must have a very clear idea of what is involved in 'research', as the word is understood by the academic historian.

Let me first of all try to say what is meant by research in this sense: research means *diligent and scholarly investigation in all the available primary and secondary sources, conducted not merely with the aim of 'making a book', but in order to extend human knowledge in a particular area.*

Now there is quite a lot here which needs explaining. First of all, the crucial distinction between primary sources and secondary sources. A primary source is a source which came into existence during the actual period of the past which the historian is studying; it is, if you like, the basic raw material out of which history (defined, let us remember once again, as 'the historian's interpretation of the past') is made. A *secondary source* is the (or any) interpretation itself, written later by the historian looking back upon a period in the past. Roughly speaking one can say that the historian's function is to convert the raw material, the primary sources, into the finished historical product, the secondary source. This 'finished product' is still a source in that it will be used by other scholars, students and ordinary people with a general interest in history.

We said above that research must involve 'investigation in *all the available primary and secondary sources'*. The idea behind the second part of this statement is that no historian should embark on any subject without first having the common sense, and the courtesy, to try to master what his colleagues have written on that same subject. He may well find many interesting leads, and indeed pieces of concrete information, from these secondary works. But this work in secondary sources, essential though it is, is perhaps best regarded as merely a prelude to the real labours of research. For we certainly would not think very highly of an historian who stopped short after reading all the relevant books written by other historians. Usually we regard work as scholarly in proportion to its dependence upon study of the raw material, the primary sources (we saw in Unit 3, in fact, that one of the great achievements of Ranke, in pioneering the modern discipline of history, was this emphasis on primary sources).

In our definition I also said that investigation in the two types of sources (primary and secondary) should be 'diligent and scholarly'. It is the main purpose of this particular unit to explain the basic methodology of the historian, which he brings to bear on his *primary sources,* and upon which he rests the claim that his work is diligent and scholarly.

There is one further point included in my definition which you need not worry too much about at the moment, but to which I shall return when, in the next unit, I discuss the value and the weakness of *pop history*. This is the point about research being concerned with expanding human knowledge, not just with 'making a book'. The difference here is one of aim and objective. The true researcher should have a genuine desire to increase human knowledge by exploring new territory. This aim is rather different from that of the author who thinks it would be rather nice to write a book, but has no particularly strong feelings on what he should write his book about, and in fact prefers to stick within the relatively easy territory of a topic which has already been explored quite fully by other historians. As we shall see later, one of the characteristics of pop history is that, very reasonably, it does not set out to increase human knowledge, but rather to communicate in a popular way knowledge which has been discovered by other historians. This knowledge discovered by other historians rests on what we can genuinely call *research*; if the author of a popular book talks about his research, he is using the word in the loose way mentioned above.

The important point is that research, truly understood, is directed towards exploring the unknown, towards *increasing* the sum of human knowledge, even if the increase may in itself seem rather small compared with the vast problems facing mankind.

It can happen that when a historian is concerned to increase knowledge on a rather large topic (such as, say, 'The Nature of Revolutions' or 'The Causes of Industrial Progress'), perhaps by illuminating new themes, or indicating new contrasts and comparisons, he will mainly depend on the secondary works of other authors; it may then still be reasonable to say that his work rests on *research*. For the moment, though, it is better that you should accept that *research*, as generally understood by historians, implies work carried out in *primary sources*.

This brings us back, then, to the point that we must be absolutely clear about the distinction between a *primary source* and a *secondary source*.

EXERCISE

Here are titles, or descriptions, of various sources, primary and secondary, for the history of sixteenth-century Europe. In the box provided place a *P* against the primary sources, and an *S* against the secondary sources.

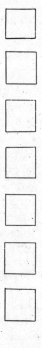

1 A. G. Dickens, *The Age of Humanism and Reformation*, (first published 1972).

2 *Journals of the House of Lords*, 1510–1614.

3 Reports of the Venetian Ambassadors to the Venetian Senate, covering the years 1496–1533.

4 John Knox, *The History of the Reformation in Scotland* (first published 1587).

5 H. G. Koenigsberger and George L. Mosse, *Europe in the Sixteenth Century* (first published 1968).

6 N. Machiavelli, *The Prince* (completed in 1516, first published 1530).

7 M. Weber, 'Die Protestantische Ethik und der Geist des Kapitalismus' ('The Protestant Ethic and the Spirit of Capitalism') in *Archiv für Sozialwissenschaft und Sozialpolitik (Archives of Social History and Social Politics)*, Volume XX, 1904.

ANSWERS

1	S	3	P	5	S
2	P	4	P	6	P
				7	S

DISCUSSION

If you have understood section 1 you should have got all of these right. The Ps are 'raw material' originating in the sixteenth century itself; the Ss are later interpretations. Source 7, no doubt, is a *difficult* source, coming from a German academic journal published in 1904; nonetheless it is still quite definitely a *secondary* source. Source 4, is slightly tricky too: as a contemporary history (see section 3, p. 66) it contains elements of secondary interpretation as well as John Knox's own primary experiences. But basically it is a primary source. If you are in any doubt at all about all this, read section 1 again.

EXERCISE

Which of these two passages shows more evidence of genuine research? Indicate your answer in your notebook, and add a brief note on the reasons for your choice.

1   The series of acts of parliament denying the authority of the Pope which were passed in the 1530s, brought two political consequences. The unprecedented flurry of activity brought a new power and status to parliament: by 1558, for example, the formal request for Freedom of Speech, previously a dubious right, was regularly included in the Speaker's petition at the beginning of each parliament. The second, and major, consequence was the emergence of England as what we would now call an 'independent nation state'. This is apparent from the very language of the various acts of parliament – for example the Act of Annates which states: 'This realm of England is an Empire, and so hath been accepted in the world . . .'

2   According to the Victorian historians, 1485 was a key date in English history when, following upon a century of civil war, Henry VII succeeded in establishing strong 'modern' government, what the historian J. R. Green called the 'new monarchy'. Such twentieth-century historians as A. F. Pollard played down 1485 as a key date, stressing the similarities between Henry VII's methods and those of his predecessors. More recently Professor G. R. Elton, while accepting the idea of continuity as between Henry VII and his predecessors, has put forward the notion of a break in the 1530s, when 'modern' government really came into being.

Figure 1   Manuscript Room of the British Museum: scholars consulting manuscript primary sources (Reproduced by permission of the British Library Board).

Figure 2   Reading room of the British Museum: students and scholars consulting printed primary and secondary sources (Reproduced by permission of the British Library Board).

SPECIMEN ANSWER

Passage 1. Reasons: 1 actually includes references to, and material directly drawn from, such primary sources as Acts of Parliament, Speaker's petitions, etc. The point made by 1 may be dubious, and 2 may be a more useful survey: but 2 clearly is based only on secondary works by Green, Pollard, etc. (As a piece of *historiography*, that is to say 'history of historical writing', 2 could be termed a work of research in that Green, Pollard etc. then become primary sources for the historical writing of the time – but ignore this point if you find it difficult.)

Remembering what was said about *primary sources* in the previous section see (in the next exercise) how many kinds of primary source you can think of yourself. (You will find television programme 4 *The historian and his sources: Stratford case study* and radio programme 4 *Handling primary sources: women in the First World War* useful here.)

EXERCISE

In your notebook list as many primary sources as you can think of. Either just list them as they occur to you, or, if you feel up to it, try to organize the sources systematically into different categories.

Figure 3 Ancient Greek coins (Reproduced by permission of the Trustees of the British Museum).

Figure 4 *Building inscription from Hadrian's Wall (Museum of Antiquities, University of Newcastle-upon-Tyne).*

SPECIMEN ANSWER

Record sources

Central government sources

Government edicts, laws, charters, records of exchequer, chancery and other government departments. Records of parliaments, estates or other representative institutions. Council and cabinet records, ambassadors reports, diplomatic dispatches. Records of central law courts, central police records.

Local records

Manorial records, local legal cases and reports (including for instance reports of the Inquisition), parish registers, local police reports, parish poor relief records, local government records, local electoral records (e.g. poll books).

Other formal records

University records, records of societies, records of political parties, trade union minutes and reports.

Private business records

Estate records, wage returns, contracts, prospectuses, minutes of board meetings etc.

Official surveys and reports

Domesday Book, reports of commissions etc.

Chronicles and histories

Monastic chronicles, 'chivalric' chronicles, town chronicles, civic histories and other contemporary histories and memoirs.

Family and personal sources

Letters, diaries.

Polemical and media

Pamphlets, treatises and polemical writings, sermons, newspapers, cartoons, etchings and other illustrative material, films, radio tapes, television tapes.

Archaeology, industrial archaeology, etc.

Inscriptions, entire or part remains (buildings, walls, etc.), pots and other artefacts, coins, paper money, entire or part remains of factories, old machinery, work-people's houses, remains of transportation systems, furniture.

Literary and artistic sources

Novels, romances etc., plays, poems, philosophical writings, painting, sculpture, architecture.

Other sources

Place names, maps, aerial photography, photographs, oral traditions (folk songs, etc.), posters and advertisements, blood groups, statistics.

DISCUSSION

You may not have listed as many entries as I have given here, and you probably will not have organized the sources in the way I have. If you have got more entries, congratulations. And if you have found a better way of breaking up the categories of sources, still heartier congratulations. In fact, there is no satisfactory way that I know of of categorizing different types of source materials. But let's leave that for a second, while you pause to try to absorb this great range of historical 'raw material'.

However, even so, it must be stressed that this is by no means a complete list; without doubt one could think of many other items worthy of inclusion (and perhaps you have done so). To put the matter at its simplest, *anything* which came into existence during the particular period which the historian is studying is a primary source for that period. Obviously, in terms of sheer practicality and utility, a line will have to be drawn somewhere. Thus the wrapping paper of a bar of chocolate will be in the strictest sense a primary source for the future historian studying the age in which we now live; on the other hand since there will be such a wealth of other primary sources we could easily forgive the future historian for ignoring the chocolate wrapper on the grounds that it is completely insignificant compared with these other sources.

Now, I don't suppose for one moment you broke up your list of sources into the sorts of category ('record sources', 'family and personal' etc.) that I have done. Quite possibly you produced a very brief and miscellaneous list of individual sources. Perhaps you even included some overlap, such as putting down both private papers, and diaries, letters, receipts etc., which of course make up private papers. Anyway it is all rather difficult, and there is certainly no agreed principle of categorization among historians. Let me, however, now look at each of my headings in turn. Basically by *record sources* I mean sources which formally record a decision whether taken by one ruler, such as a king or emperor, or by a group of people such as a council or a parliament; in the latter case, record sources also formally note the discussions and proceedings. I have made a rough, and fairly obvious distinction between records of central government, local government, and records of other institutions (though of course there is considerable variation in the significance of these differences over time). Just as I have included documents relating to government business transactions as record sources, so also I have included documents relating to private and business transactions: these all are, or purport to be, records of something which definitely happened.

Then I move on to *official surveys and reports*. Such documents come into existence when a government or some other institution or individual sets out to collect information. Included here also are compilations of information, such as, in our own day, directories and handbooks. These are of course records in a sense too, but they do not record actual decisions or transactions, but are rather the result of surveys or inquiries, or are simply collections of information.

Next came *chronicles and histories*. Of course, to qualify as primary sources these must be contemporary with the period being studied. In fact it was very common, first for monks, then later for lay commentators, to compile chronicles, or write histories of their own time. Such sources are not much used in modern history, but they are very valuable for the mediaeval period, and indeed for the Renaissance period.

Family and personal sources could of course include the sort of business transactions I have listed separately. But as the detailed list shows, I'm thinking here of things like personal letters, private diaries and so on, which, obviously, are less a direct record of transactions or listing of information.

My next heading is *polemical and media*. Obviously there is a distinction between polemical tracts which are designed very forcefully to put one point of view, and newspapers whose basic purpose may well be the objective dissemination of information. However, as we all know, most newspapers do indeed have a pretty definite political point of view.

Archaeology, industrial archaeology, etc.: the uses of such sources for very early periods are fairly well known. We can learn a lot about more modern periods too, particularly about lifestyles and living conditions, from, for example, household utensils, furniture and surviving buildings. Pay particular attention to this section of television programme 4.

Literary and artistic sources: architecture, novels, poems, painting, sculpture, all take their place as fundamental products of the age which the historian is studying; if he does not pay attention to them, he will fail to understand that age in its total aspect. On the other hand, such creative artefacts of a past age do raise certain problems which are perhaps not always too well understood; for this reason we shall turn again to this problem in section 4.

Other sources: with advances in the techniques of history, new kinds of sources are constantly being brought into use; indeed we might well say that the most obvious sign of progress in historical study is the way in which more and more sources, of ever-changing appearance and content, are brought in for systematic study by the historian. Yet it is sometimes a little difficult to know where to draw the line between something which has actual existence as a *source,* and something which is really more properly described as a *technique.* On the list given above, both place names and aerial photography obviously do not have a real existence dating back, say, to the thirteenth century, though they are often used as sources for the study of thirteenth-century villages. The taking of an aerial photograph is in fact a technique for making clear the contours (that is, the outlines of former areas of cultivation, paths, remains of old buildings, etc.) of a mediaeval village which have survived from the thirteenth century to our own time, but which are not readily apparent to someone standing on the ground. Perhaps, if we are to be absolutely accurate, we should say that the real *primary source* is the remaining contour and relics of the village; while the taking of the aerial photograph is merely a modern *technique* for making more use of this particular source.

The question of *place names* is an even more complicated one; in some cases a name has survived right through the centuries, and it is from this name that the historian deduces something significant about the original place. (Good examples of this are surviving place names with such distinctively Scandinavian endings as *-by,* as in Whitby, and *-thorpe,* as in Scunthorpe, which give the historian a very good idea of the extent of Viking settlement in England.) In other cases names have changed in a rather subtle way and the historian has to try to puzzle out what these changes are, before he can start making his deductions. (A simple example of this is Chiswell Street, the site of the old Whitbread brewery: this name *may* imply that there was once a 'choice well' here.) Obviously, anyway, the name of a village does not have the same kind of concrete existence as say a Royal Charter, or a private diary: the name may be on a signboard, but it is rather unlikely that that signboard will have survived from the time of the origins of the village. On the other hand the actual name will not be confined to one signboard, but will probably be found in all sorts of different maps, charters, books, etc. The real primary sources might be held to be these various maps, books, signboards, plus, perhaps, oral traditions about the name, and pronunciations of the name, so that we might prefer again to regard the study of place names as a *technique.* And this would be entirely reasonable since the study of place names, though vitally useful to the historian, is really a branch of an older academic discipline, *philology.*

Two further examples of this difficult borderline between source and technique (out of many) are, firstly, *serology,* and, secondly, *statistics.* Serology is a technique used particularly in studying the tribal history of Africa, where there is a great shortage of the more traditional type of written source: basically it involves the study of blood groups. Here one might well say that it is the living human being, or even his blood, which, if anything, is the primary source; and that again serology is simply a technique.

Statistics, in the form of, say, pages of royal revenues, or estate accounts, or details of a country's balance of payments over several years, clearly do have a concrete physical existence like other types of primary source. But, most usually, what happens is that the historian pulls out the statistics from quite a wide range of different kinds of source – such as published government records, private contracts, private estate records, wage returns and so on. Unless in fact the historian is lucky enough to light upon page after page of recognizable primary material which in fact consists almost entirely of statistical information, then statistics is rather a technique which he brings to bear on a variety of sources, than a particular source as such. (And even where there is genuine statistical *material,* the historian will still have to *apply* statistical *techniques* to get any meaning out of it.)

This perhaps seems a little complicated. The main thing, once again, is to grasp the essential point about the fantastic *variety* of primary sources which the historian may use. Leaving these complications aside, and also the ones arising from any attempt to categorize different types of source, I want, in introducing the important distinction between witting and unwitting testimony to look again at some of the sources I have listed whose relevance is mainly for the periods before the Renaissance.

Clearly for the earlier forms of human society, for which very little remains in the way of written records, the various types of *archaeological source* will be particularly important. The *inscriptions* will be useful for the study of politics and public affairs; but pots and other artefacts (*artefact* is a convenient word used to describe any object made by man, and it includes sculpture and painting, as well as utilitarian and mechanical objects) will be useful for the study of the conditions of ordinary life.

Coins have all sorts of subtle uses. Sometimes the actual illustrations and inscriptions on them tell us something about what matters seemed significant to the particular society which used the coins. The Roman emperors used coins for disseminating propaganda. More often coins serve as a basic source of precise information which can help to illuminate the significance of a whole host of other archaeological finds. For example, they may help to fix the date of a site which is being dug.

We might well have made *papyri* a separate heading. Papyrus was one of the main writing materials used in the ancient Mediterranean world (paper, as yet, being unknown there), and all kinds of documents (if we make a distinction by *content*) written on papyrus have survived: both statements of laws and practices relating to religious groups and also private accounts of individual families.

In the list of sources in section 2 I specifically identified one of the most famous of all English mediaeval documents, Domesday Book. Under the heading of Royal Charters, I might also have mentioned Magna Carta, a statement of the rights granted by King John to his nobles in 1215. Such documents, note, tell us about public matters, the activities of kings and great men; though the great and unique virtue of Domesday Book is that, although it was drawn up to serve the

Figure 5 Magna Carta facsimile. From the original Cotton Ms Augustus 11106 (Reproduced by permission of the British Library Board).

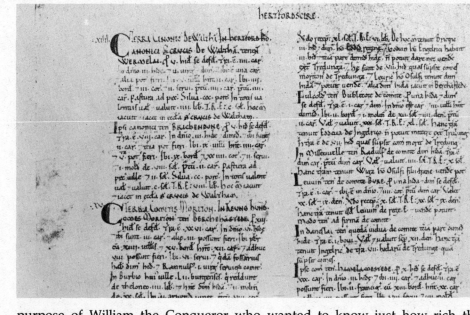

Figure 6   Excerpt from the Domesday Book, fol.135^d (Public Record Office).

purpose of William the Conqueror who wanted to know just how rich the country he had conquered was, in fact it gives us a fascinating insight into the structure and life of the various communities of eleventh century England. (To compile Domesday Book, William sent his investigators to every part of England to collect details of every village from the sworn testimony of local men – details about who held what land and about the value of each holding and its stock.) Magna Carta, too, tells us a little at least about the humbler people of thirteenth century England, and a good deal about the general assumptions held by leading members of society at that time.

And now is the time to introduce you to what I believe to be a crucial distinction in the types of evidence which a historian derives from his primary sources. On the one hand we have what I call *witting testimony*, on the other *unwitting testimony*. Witting testimony is the information which the person who originally compiled the document intended it to convey. If it is a record of a debate in the king's council, that formal record of the debate is the witting testimony. If it is a law defining the relationships between the nobles and the peasants, these relationships are the witting testimony of the document. But the first document may, *unwittingly*, tell us something about the way in which council debates were conducted, something about the assumptions held by members of that particular council; perhaps something about the relationship between councillors and the king. None of this information was intended for contemporary readers: they would probably know it anyway. But it may be very valuable information for the historian trying to understand the nature of a particular society in the past and its institutions. Similarly with the second document the law will tell the historian that it was fully assumed at the time that there would be a clear distinction between nobles and peasants; again contemporaries would take this for granted, but it could be valuable information for the historian. There, then, is this important distinction between the witting testimony, the message the document deliberately set out to convey for contemporaries (also of course of immense importance to the historian), and the unwitting testimony, useful evidence which the historian may derive from the document despite the deliberate intentions of the creators of the document.

EXERCISE

Now read back through the previous five paragraphs where I have given examples of the sorts of things historians get from various sources from archaeology to Domesday Book and Magna Carta. Which of the pieces of information I mention fall into the category of witting testimony, and which into the category of unwitting testimony?

Figure 7   Allhusen Works, Gateshead, 1907. Photo from G. G. Walmsley. The Struggle for Supremacy, *1907. Industrial archaeology or photographic evidence?*

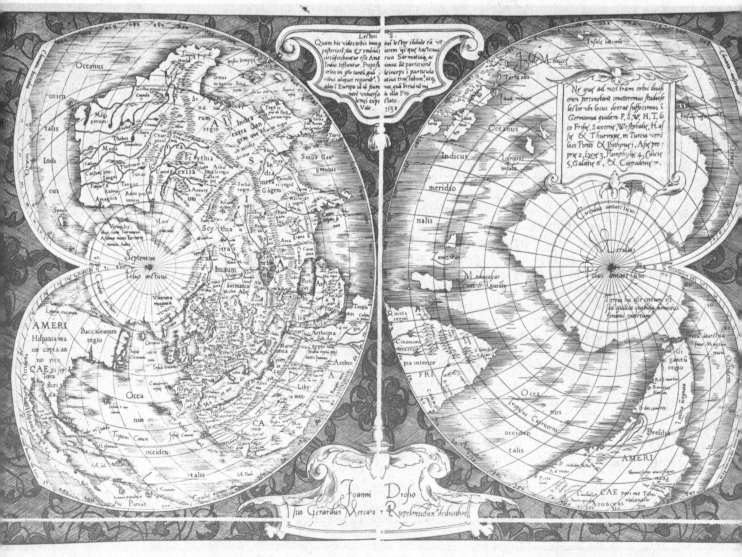

Figure 8   Facsimile copy of the world map of Gerardus Mercator, 1538 (Map Division, Library of Congress).

[This Document is the Property of His Britannic Majesty's Government.] 188

Printed for the War Cabinet. June 1918.

SECRET.

77

WAR CABINET, **434**.

Minutes of a Meeting of the War Cabinet held at 10, Downing Street, S.W., on Friday, June 21, 1918, at 11 A.M.

Present:

The Right Hon. A. BONAR LAW, M.P. (*in the Chair*).

The Right Hon. the EARL CURZON OF KEDLESTON, K.G., G.C.S.I., G.C.I.E.

The Right Hon. G. N. BARNES, M.P.

Lieutenant-General the Right Hon. J. C. SMUTS, K.C.

The Right Hon. A. CHAMBERLAIN, M.P.

The following were also present:—

The Right Hon. SIR A. STANLEY, M.P., President, Board of Trade (for Minutes 1, 2, 3, 4).

SIR STEPHENSON KENT, K.C.B., Ministry of Munitions (for Minute 5).

SIR L. WORTHINGTON EVANS, Bart., M.P., Parliamentary Secretary, Ministry of Munitions (for Minutes 1, 4, 5).

SIR G. CALTHROP, Bart., Coal Controller (for Minutes 1 to 4).

The Right Hon. W. BRACE, M.P., Parliamentary Under-Secretary for Home Affairs (for Minute 5).

SIR A. D. HALL, K.C.B., M.A., F.R.S., Permanent Secretary, Board of Agriculture and Fisheries (for Minute 5).

Lieutenant-Colonel W. DALLY JONES, C.M.G., *Acting Secretary.*

Mr. THOMAS JONES, *Assistant Secretary.*

Captain L. F. BURGIS, *Assistant Secretary.*

Lieutenant-Colonel L. WILSON, C.M.G., D.S.O., M.P., *Assistant Secretary.*

Coal Rationing.

1. THE War Cabinet had before them a memorandum by the President of the Board of Trade with regard to the order for rationing household fuel and light (Paper G.T.-4889).

Sir Albert Stanley stated that there was one correction to be made in his memorandum. In paragraph 3, the first line after the scale, there should be added "up to a maximum of 20 tons" after the words "larger houses." Sir Albert Stanley continued that the new regulations, as proposed in his memorandum, were in reality an extension of the Coal Rationing Order, which was applied to the London area last year. The new regulations would, however, apply to the whole country except Ireland, but the rationing would be on a reduced scale. The rationing of gas and electric light was also included in the order. In reply to a question as to how the new order would affect the larger houses, both in London and the country, Sir Albert Stanley said that this was met by taking into consideration the size of the rooms. A room of more than 4,000 cubic feet would count as two rooms, and a room of 8,000 cubic feet would count as three rooms. There was also the opportunity to appeal for a special assessment.

[1365—434]

Figure 9 Excerpt from War Cabinet minutes, June 1918 (Reproduced by permission of the Controller, Her Majesty's Stationery Office).

SPECIMEN ANSWER

Inscriptions useful for the study of politics and public affairs – witting testimony.

Pots useful for study of conditions of ordinary life – unwitting testimony (pots were certainly not created to tell a future historian, or for that matter contemporaries, about the conditions of life).

Coins useful for what matters seemed most significant to the particular society which used them – unwitting testimony.

Coins used for disseminating propaganda – witting testimony.

Papyrus as statements of laws and practices and as private accounts – both witting and unwitting testimony (the actual laws, the actual accounts of transactions, are witting testimony; the assumptions which lie behind these are the unwitting testimony).

Domesday Book and Magna Carta tell us about public matters and activities of kings – mainly witting, but some unwitting testimony (again, what the documents actually state are the witting testimony, the assumptions that lie behind these statements are the unwitting testimony).

Domesday Book and how rich the country was – witting testimony.

Insight into the structure of life – mainly unwitting testimony, though I suppose it could be said that in part the document does consciously do this.

Details of who held what land, etc. – witting testimony.

Magna Carta tells us a little about the humbler people of the thirteenth century – both witting and unwitting testimony.

General assumptions held by leading members of society – unwitting testimony.

Now I want to say something more about the change and expansion in the nature of primary source materials during the period of the Renaissance and Reformation. During the fourteenth, fifteenth and sixteenth centuries government became more elaborate and sophisticated. As in other matters, the Italian city states in the fourteenth century were the pioneers, and it was here that the official known as the Secretary (ancestor of the future Secretary of State) first appeared. Through him much documentation was created. In Rome, as capital of the Catholic Church, a very complex administration developed and the enormous archives of the papacy form a central source for European history of the period. For England in the sixteenth century we have full collections of state papers, statutes, and journals of both House of Lords and House of Commons. Also in Italy there began the accumulation of foreign dispatches and diplomatic documents. Reports from the Venetian ambassadors were in fact one of the basic primary sources which Ranke used in his first book, *History of the Latin and German Peoples, 1494–1514*; these reports which poured into Venice while it was still one of the great commercial powers in Europe, gave all sorts of information about the various European countries.

During the late middle ages monastic chronicles tended to give way to 'chivalric' chronicles, whose emphasis was very much on battles, and indeed on diplomatic relations and foreign policy. These in turn, especially in Italy, gave way to town chronicles, in which the pride of the early Renaissance Italian city states was celebrated. These in turn give way to more rounded civic histories, and then to other types of contemporary history, often of course with a strong political element, written by such famous Italian Renaissance figures as Leonardo Bruni and Nicholo Machiavelli (see what Dickens has to say about these two writers). With the spread of education and Renaissance culture, private collections of letters became more important in the sixteenth century; and autobiographies and memoirs, which were fairly rare in the fifteenth century, became quite common in the sixteenth century. Especially outstanding, particularly for the evidence it gives for social and artistic life in Italy and France, is the *Autobiography* of the great sculptor Benvenuto Cellini (1500–71).

The controversies of the Reformation, aided of course by the dissemination of printing presses, created an enormous historical literature of theological and philosophical writing, polemical tracts, and contemporary histories such as John Knox's *History of the Reformation in Scotland*. The opinions of humble illiterate Protestants are harder to discover: one useful source is the proceedings of heretics put on trial.

A proportion of this vast new source material created in the period of Renaissance and Reformation was made available in printed form by devoted scholars from the nineteenth century onwards. Obviously it is preferable for historians to consult the actual original document in its archive; but scholars of the Renaissance of necessity have to do much of their work in the published collections of original documentation.

Now the other major historical period which you will be studying in this course is that of industrialization in nineteenth century Britain.

EXERCISE

What new sources do you think came into being during this period of industrialization?

SPECIMEN ANSWER

Basically the changes arise from a further development in the nature of government, particularly the extension of government interest into social and economic matters; from the very technological innovations of industrialization, and from the growing complexity of the new society created by industrialization, including the growth of democracy and the working class movement.

Thus government surveys, census reports, reports of Royal Commissions, and so on become very important. So do trade union papers and police reports. Newspapers expand in influence and importance. Indeed there is an expansion in nearly all the main types of source, for example parliamentary debates. Industrial archaeology now becomes an important source.

Industrial archaeology, it may be noted, can be very useful in studying economic history in general, and more specifically in studying the history of a particular industry, or of a particular locality. Surviving written records may give practically no guidance as to what particular inventions or machines actually looked like, and how they actually operated: in such a case the discovery of the actual remains of a particular machine or invention can be of critical importance.

Place names and aerial photography I have already said something about. A photograph taken today of some industrial or other remains, obviously, like aerial photography, is the product of a *technique* rather than a source in its own right. But photographs which were actually taken in the nineteenth century, or early in the twentieth century, may be very valuable primary sources, giving us a clear idea about what certain things looked like, which we could not get from written sources (photographs may also tell us about *attitudes* – that is their unwitting testimony: sometimes they make a deliberate social comment – that is their witting testimony). Film material dating back to the early twentieth century, clearly, will have this use as well. But old newsreels can tell us more than this: in fact in the age of the developing mass media, the newsreel film (and, in our own day, the television film) begins to take on many of the functions which once belonged exclusively to the newspaper. It would still be true to say that the historian studying the twentieth century will probably find most of his information in written and printed sources, but there are times when archive film can yield additional bits of information not readily obtainable elsewhere. For example, newsreel film of the suffragette agitation before the First World War sometimes gives a clearer insight into contemporary attitudes towards the suffragettes and clearer insight into the sorts of things contemporaries found significant about the suffragette movement, than do surviving newspaper accounts.

The study of oral traditions, folk songs, and so on again moves us towards the realm of specialized techniques, though they are also in their own right genuine, if often somewhat elusive, primary sources. No historian would willingly base his interpretation of past events purely on folk song, or other oral material; but many historians have been led to investigate further in the more conventional sources because they have received an initial *lead* from some episode, or name, mentioned in a folk song. And again of course sources of this type can give invaluable insight into the attitudes, prejudices and styles of thought of the people of the age from which folk song or tradition derives (unwitting testimony once more).

EXERCISE

Listed below are three historical topics related to the period of the Renaissance and Reformation, with one related to the period of industrialization, and one to the present day. Note down three of the main sorts of sources which you think would be useful to the historian in studying each of these topics. If you feel able to add any comments about what will be witting testimony and what unwitting please do so: but don't worry too much about that – the exercise is quite difficult anyway!

1 Social life in fourteenth and fifteenth century Florence.
2 Henry VIII and the Reformation in England.
3 The social, political and religious outlook of William Shakespeare.
4 English coal miners in the early nineteenth century.
5 The impact of the Open University on higher education in Britain in the early 1970s.

Figure 10   Aerial photography: view of Nun Coltham, Lincolnshire (Aerofilms Ltd).

Figure 11   Newsreel still: mass meeting of Suffragettes in Trafalgar Square, 1910 (Photo: National Film Archive; reproduced by courtesy of EMI/Pathe Film Library).

SPECIMEN ANSWERS AND DISCUSSION

1   I can think of a number of major types of source. I hope you have got at least three of them. First of all, there are the contemporary histories, particularly that of Bruni. Then there are the official records of the Florentine state. What these two sources deliberately or formally tell us is their witting testimony; the assumptions and attitudes which lie beneath – an important part of social life – are the unwitting testimony. After that come the surviving private papers of individual Florentine citizens: when one person is writing to another (just as someone might do today) about a festival he or she had attended – that is important witting testimony. Any assumption revealed – for example about the central and unquestioned role of the Church – is unwitting testimony. But I hope also you thought of the philosophical, literary, artistic, and architectural creations of the Florentine Renaissance. And, finally, with a well preserved city like Florence, one can learn a lot just by going back and visiting the place as it is today. Mainly unwitting testimony all that – since these things were really created for purposes rather different from that of a historian studying the social life of fourteenth and fifteenth century Florence.

2   The Statutes, or Acts of Parliament, are the formal witting way through which Henry VIII carried out the Reformation. To see the other end of things, it might be worth consulting the papal archives. Then, of course, there are all the religious tracts. Local church records would be helpful, and further information could be derived from the journals of both houses of Parliament. This is one of the well-worn topics of history textbooks, and is in fact one for which there is quite a wealth of documentary source material, very largely, for a clear-cut political topic like this, witting testimony.

3   The opposite is true for Shakespeare where the sources are sparse and we are very dependent on unwitting testimony. A major source would have to be his plays and poems. There are no personal or family archives as such, though, as television programme 4 shows, there are one or two references to him in contemporary record documents. Beyond that we would have to depend largely on what contemporaries said about him – that would be witting testimony.

4 (a) Government surveys and reports on mining conditions (mainly witting testimony, though also unwittingly revealing attitudes);
(b) miners' union records (witting and unwitting);
(c) industrial archaeology (unwitting testimony);
(d) comments of private individuals on mining and mining conditions (witting and unwitting testimony).

5 The obvious sources would be:
(a) Internal Open University archives, together with course material, and accounts written by members of Open University staff. (Course material is a marvellous example of unwitting testimony in this context. My witting purpose in writing these units is to help you to learn the basic principles of historical study. Unwittingly I am probably giving away all sorts of information about my own assumptions and prejudices. Think what a future historian might do with it!)
(b) Internal materials from other universities and institutions of higher education.
(c) Department of Education materials relating to the Open University.
(d) Comments in the educational journals and in the press (witting testimony in their factual descriptions of our system, but unwitting testimony in revealing changes in opinion – originally pretty hostile – towards the Open University).

4 CRITICISM AND EVALUATION OF PRIMARY SOURCES

Theoretically, the first point a historian must establish about any primary source he is dealing with is its *authenticity*. That is he must establish that the document really is what it purports to be, that, say, a tract purporting to be written by Luther really was written by Luther, not by an imitator or a detractor, or that a charter issued by the French King Henry IV to the town of Rouen, really was issued by Henry IV, not forged later, say, by the citizens of the town wishing to create special privileges for themselves. But in reality, most of the documents which working historians use are well vouched for; it is only occasionally that a new document is discovered where strict tests for authenticity have to be carried out. So, for the purposes of this Foundation Course work, we shall take it that all documents which you are studying have had their authenticity fully established.

Taking authenticity as established, there are then a series of basic questions which the historian must ask of every source he has to deal with.

The reason for asking these questions is to establish the value and reliability of the source for the particular topic the historian is working on. Of course the professional historian will tend to raise many of these questions instinctively without having to work his way systematically through them as I want you to do (obviously, if he goes to a collection of letters, or of statutes for example, he is likely to know in advance what type of source he is about to consult). Yet these questions are implicit in his work all the same, and it is very important that you should master them.

The questions are:

1   What type of source is it? A private letter? A Royal Charter, or what?

2   What person, or group of persons, created the source in the first place? What basic attitudes, prejudices, etc. would he/they be likely to have? (For example if the author of the document was a known Protestant activist – e.g. John Knox – this might give rise to certain biases.) If the document is that of a miners' trade union it might (*might!*) be unfairly hostile to the coal owners.

3   How and for what purpose did the document come into existence? For instance if a Royal Charter was it granted out of the King's free will, or was it extracted from him under duress? If a letter, was it written with the genuine intention of conveying reliable information, or, say, to curry favour with the recipient (knowledge of the respective social positions of the writer and recipient would be helpful). If a contemporary history, was it merely written to make money? Involved in this question then is: who was it written or addressed *to*, or who was it written for?

4   How far is the author of the source really in a good position to provide first-hand information on the particular topic the historian is interested in? Is the writer dependent, say, on hearsay? A middle class intellectual in the early nineteenth century writing on mining conditions might not really be in a very good position to give us authoritative information. If an Ambassador reports home that a revolution is likely in the country to which he is accredited, we have to be sure that he has some real evidence and is not just swayed by wishful thinking, or stupid panic.

5   The historian has to be sure he has properly understood the document as contemporaries would have understood it. This is where the various technical skills of the historian come in.

(a) There's the problem of deciphering inscriptions, hieroglyphics and certain types of handwriting (even just plain bad handwriting). We won't inflict any of these problems on you.

71

(b) There are the problems of archaic or foreign languages. Within the Renaissance period key documents are written in classical Greek and classical Latin, but also in Mediaeval Latin, which is slightly different. Many other documents are written in difficult vernacular dialects. Even the English to be understood is the English of the Renaissance period.

(c) Apart from the general linguistic problem, there is the problem of specific technical or semi-technical phrases, or special esoteric allusions in the source. Thus when an Elizabethan document refers to the Star Chamber, we have to know exactly what the Star Chamber was. When we try to read a Renaissance letter we have to understand all the references to classical mythology which we are likely to find in it. We have to understand all references, all allusions, all obscurities.

EXERCISE

With regard to this point of understanding language as contemporaries understood it, what did John Knox mean by 'regiment' in his famous sermon against 'The Monstrous Regiment of Women'?

ANSWER

You'll find the answer in *The Age of Humanism and Reformation*.

6   If there are any other persons (or places, institutions or books or works of art, etc.) referred to in the text of the source, then in order to make the document as clear and as meaningful to us as possible, we would want to know exactly who or what they are, and why they are mentioned.

7   There is a further question which is generally of relevance to archaeological sources, or artefacts such as paintings, rather than to traditional written sources: that is – where was the source found? If a Mediterranean pot is found in London, that gives the pot a special added significance. So too if a letter from one trade unionist to another was actually discovered in a police file. But this takes us into an area which need not usually concern you in connection with the examples of source material you will be encountering.

In studying any document the professional historian will, of course, bring to bear on it what he already knows of the period and topic from his studies in other sources, primary and secondary. The more you already know about a subject, the more you can squeeze out of a document relating to that subject.

Now in this part of the course I cannot expect you to have much background historical knowledge, though I hope you are acquiring a little on the Renaissance. You will mainly be asked about the basic principles of source criticism, the fundamental questions the historian must always ask.

But the whole point of all this perhaps slightly finicky-seeming business is to get to what the document contributes (both as *witting* and *unwitting* testimony) in the way of information, illumination or insight, or in suggesting further lines of enquiry to be followed up. (It should, incidentally, be noted that professional historians tend to consult whole ranges of documents, rather than one single, short, isolated document. I shall return to this point in contrasting the historian's activities with that of the literary scholar studying a short poem.)

EXERCISE

Imagine you are doing research in early Renaissance History and you are studying this letter dating from 1492 written by Marsilio Ficino to Paul of Middleburg.

What the poets once sang of the four ages, lead, iron, silver, and gold, our Plato in the *Republic* transferred to the four talents of men, assigning to some talents a certain leaden quality implanted in them by nature, to others iron, to others silver, and to still others gold. If then we are to call any age golden, it is beyond doubt that age which brings forth golden talents in different places. That such is true of this our age he who wishes to consider the illustrious discoveries of this century will hardly doubt. For this century, like a golden age, has restored to light the liberal arts, which were almost extinct: grammar, poetry, rhetoric, painting, sculpture, architecture, music, the ancient singing of songs to the Orphic lyre, and all this in Florence. Achieving what had been honoured among the ancients, but almost forgotten since, the age has joined wisdom with eloquence, and prudence with the military art, and this most strikingly in Federigo, Duke of Urbino, as if proclaimed in the presence of Pallas herself, and it has made his son and his brother the heirs of his virtue. In you also, my dear Paul, this century appears to have perfected astronomy, and in Florence it has recalled the Platonic teaching from darkness into light. In Germany in our times have been invented the instruments for printing books, and those tables in which in a single hour (if I may speak thus) the whole face of the heavens for an entire century is revealed, and one may mention also the Florentine machine which shows the daily motions of the heavens.

What questions (with specific reference to points in the text of the document) should we first ask about this source? Some of the answers are obvious and you may be able to add some others from your reading of chapter 1 of *The Age of Humanism and Reformation*. But the vital thing for the moment is to get the *questions* right.

Figure 12 Florence today: the Renaissance cathedral and, in front to the right, the late mediaeval fortress, the Bargello (Mansell Collection).

SPECIMEN ANSWERS

1 *What type of source?* It is a private letter.

2 *Who created it?* The letter was written by Marsilio Ficino. We learn from Dickens (pp. 32–3 – remember the index if all else fails!) that he was a protégé of Cosimo de' Medici, the virtual ruler of Florence, and the son of his physician. Ficino's house became the centre of an enthusiastic group of Platonist scholars and Ficino himself translated all Plato's *Dialogues*, wrote a commentary on Plato's *Symposium* and an original work *The Platonic Theology*.

What prejudices etc? We might expect Ficino, as a Florentine, to be biased in favour of Florence. Obviously, also, he was a fairly committed enthusiast for Plato. Possibly (I can only say *possibly*, because we'd need much more evidence on this slightly speculative point) as the son of a physician he might be unduly respectful towards such princely figures as Cosimo de' Medici, to whom, anyway, he was deeply indebted.

3   *How and why was it written, and to whom?* We have seen that before the days of the institutionalization of scholarship and science it was common for scholars to exchange ideas with each other in letters. It seems reasonable to assume that this letter was written with the genuine intention of conveying what Ficino believes to be true (not *necessarily* exactly the same as reliable information of course). Furthermore, there seems to be a genuine note of affection as between Ficino and Paul, also suggesting that he would write genuinely.

4   *How far does it provide good first-hand information?* We know that Ficino was right at the centre of intellectual developments in Florence, so he is a very good source for these. Possibly his knowledge of German developments was less good.

5   *Technical points, contemporary allusions, etc?* There are a lot of these which, to get the full contemporary meaning and flavour of the document, we would have to follow up (or which, naturally, we would already understand if – unlike me! – we were historical experts on the early Renaissance).

(a)   Who are the poets in the first line?

(b)   What is the exact reference to Plato's *Republic*?

(c)   What is the full implication of the phrase 'liberal arts'?

(d)   What is the force of the (classical) allusion to Pallas?

(e)   What exactly is Platonic teaching?

(f)   If 'instruments for printing books' are obvious, what are the 'tables' and the 'Florentine machine' also referred to? (Though he puts all three in the same breath, we today would see printing as far more important than the various astronomical devices upon which Renaissance scholars set such store.)

6   *Other names?* Well, we have Federigo, Duke of Urbino, together with his son and brother. We *might* take this reference to suggest again a certain obsequiousness towards rank on the part of Ficino. From Dickens (p. 125) we can discover (if we didn't already know) that Urbino was one of the smallest Italian city states, that Federigo and his son were great scholars, and that Federigo provided the model for Castiglione's famous *Book of the Courtier* (see Dickens p. 33) – a work which, among other things, greatly influenced Elizabethan ideas about the Renaissance gentleman.

So we move to the really important question: what do we learn from the document? I hope you have seen how, through our series of systematic questions, we have already moved some way towards answering this.

EXERCISE

1   What is the main witting testimony of this document?

2   Is there any unwitting testimony?

SPECIMEN ANSWERS

1   The message that comes through loud and clear is that a leading and representative Florentine scholar of the late fifteenth century is sure that a Renaissance ('a golden age') has taken place in his century. This is a first-class piece of evidence demonstrating that men of the time were aware of a Renaissance, and that they looked back to the wisdom of 'the ancients' while believing the period in between had been something of a dark age with the liberal arts 'almost forgotten'. More than this, Ficino gives pride of place in this development to Florence (though here he may be biased, as we have noted); yet he sees Federigo (not a Florentine) as the acme of Renaissance man in all his aspects: the stress on the individual is significant since this is often seen as a major new characteristic of Renaissance thought. (We have established from Dickens that Ficino was at the centre of Florentine intellectual developments, so that it is highly unlikely that he would be

Figure 13   Duke Federigo of Urbino; fifteenth-century terracotta in the National Gallery of the Marches, Italy (Mansell Collection).

expressing an eccentric individual opinion of his own. In fact anyone studying the period would soon come across plenty of like statements.)

2   Unwitting testimony. We can see the things he (and presumably his contemporaries) *takes for granted* as being important: the liberal arts (as defined in the letter), wisdom, eloquence, prudence *and* the military art; astronomical devices equally with printing; and, above all, the constant stress on Platonic thought.

In this exercise we have come to one of the most important points in *Introduction to History*. If there is anything in it that puzzles you, work back through it again – because I am now going to try out another one on you. For this you will need your Supplementary Texts.

EXERCISE

Turn to document B1 (Preamble of the English Act Against Appeals to Rome of 1533) in your Supplementary Texts. Read the document and raise (and where possible answer) all the necessary questions, and say what the document tells you (or in other words, what its historical significance is).

Figure 14 *Thomas Cromwell, 1485–1540, a contemporary engraving (Mansell Collection).*

Figure 15 *Elizabethan House of Commons, an engraving (Mansell Collection).*

Figure 16 *Henry VIII, after Hans Holbein c. 1536 (National Portrait Gallery).*

SPECIMEN ANSWER

1 *What type of source?* This is a document of public record (see answer and discussion to the exercise on p. 59), compared with the Ficino letter which was a private source. It is, in fact, an Act of Parliament.

2 *Who created it?* Obviously the English Parliament, though the main agent was Thomas Cromwell, who, however, found willing support from the predominantly anti-clerical parliament (see Dickens p. 175). Behind Cromwell, of course, stood the needs of the King (and indeed the nation) in the clash with the Hapsburgs and the Papacy (see Dickens p. 174).

   What prejudices etc? Clearly this document will be affected by the needs of the King, the demands of national security, and the nationalist and anti-clerical sentiments of Thomas Cromwell and the Reformation Parliament. The historical account at the beginning may not, therefore, be totally accurate.

3 *How and for what purpose did the document come into existence?* As an Act of Parliament this is part of a deliberate national policy to assert the independence of England from the Papacy and, in particular, to prohibit appeals to Rome. Clearly it is an absolutely straight record of that policy.

4 *How far does it provide good first hand information?* It is, as just noted, a real and actual part of the English Reformation, though, as we also noted, it is not such a reliable first hand source when it comes to its opening historical survey.

5 *How did contemporaries understand this document?* Obviously there are a number of technical terms and allusions which need explaining. 'Empire' obviously means something nearer to nation state than what we would understand by this word. 'Provocation' is a technical term which means 'appeal to another court'. To fully understand what is being said about the English Church, and its independence from 'any exterior person or persons', it would be necessary to know something of the previous history of the Church in England (see Dickens for this). Equally, to fully comprehend the final sentence of the document it would be necessary to understand the nature of English law at this time.

6 *Any other persons, names, etc. which need elucidation?* I don't think there are any, but let me just stress again how important it is to elucidate all obscurities in a document before interpreting it.

Now to the major questions of interpretation:

1 What is the main witting testimony of the document?
2 Is there any unwitting testimony?

In this case, the two are very much bound up together. The document is explicitly asserting, and indeed legalizing, the temporal and spiritual independence of England, under its King. And the whole document is suffused with the assumptions of Thomas Cromwell and the Reformation Parliament that this should indeed be the case, and has (as they slightly inaccurately maintain) always been the case.

We don't need to make too much of a meal of this: quite simply, this is one of the most important, and relatively straightforward, documents in the English Reformation.

BRIEF EXERCISE ON VISUAL SOURCES

Consider the various illustrative sources on pages 78–80 and indicate what you think the usefulness and the weaknesses of each one, as source material for the historian, might be.

Figure 17   *'Hanging of traitors' from* The Disasters of War, 1633, *by Jacques Callot (Mansell Collection).*

Figure 18   *Photograph of World War I female munitions workers (Imperial War Museum).*

78

Figure 19   Gustav Doré, 1832–83 Over London – by rail, *an engraving (Mary Evans Picture Library).*

Figures 20 (a) and (b)   Czech Communist leaders in Prague: two photographic versions (Photographs from Arthur Marwick Historikerens kilder, *Open University/Gyldenhal. Reproduced by permission of Gyldendal, Copenhagen).*

SPECIMEN ANSWER

Figure 17   Horrifying insight into seventeenth century warfare (the Thirty Years' War, in fact), if reliable. Actually (you may not know this) Callot was himself present at such episodes, and on the whole he aimed at a pretty dispassionate record, so this is a good source.

Figure 18   Women at work; women wearing trousers. Obviously a posed photograph, but accurate enough.

Figure 19   Evidently a source for the impact of railway building, particularly on the living conditions of the poor. Possibly some propagandist intent and some artistic licence. But we can check it against other types of source: in broad spirit, if not exact detail, it's accurate.

Figures 20(a) and 20(b)   The dangers of photographic evidence! But the hostility of the official Communist establishment and the lengths they were prepared to go are only too evident.

5 LITERATURE AND ART AS PRIMARY SOURCES

The use of literature and art as historical sources raises problems which are not always fully recognized.

One obvious point must be stressed at the outset. A novel or a poem is a source for the period *in* which it was written, not for the period *about* which it was written. In other words the novels of Sir Walter Scott may tell us a good deal about the early nineteenth century when Scott himself was writing; but though Scott was undoubtedly historically-minded, his historical novels do not always give us a great deal of authentic information about the ages in which they are supposed to be set. They may tell us a little through the author's own imaginative historical insight – so that in this sense they become a kind of popularized secondary source – but they certainly are not primary sources for these ages. In the same way a Renaissance painting of the Crucifixion will be a marvellous primary source for the Renaissance, but it will in no sense be a primary source for the first century AD. Shakespeare's history plays are good sources for contemporary attitudes towards politics and society and, in particular, for Tudor attitudes to English history: they are not, obviously, primary sources for the historic Macbeth, Hamlet or Richard II.

Too ready use has sometimes been made of novels in the writing of that species of 'social history' sometimes more appropriately referred to as 'polite chat about the past'. Art and literature, being an important facet of the age which produced them, must always rank as important primary sources for the study of that age. But it is misusing literature to expect to find in it the concrete facts of everyday existence, wage rates, living standards, environmental conditions and so on. For information on these matters the historian should prefer not to take the word of the novelist (whose first concern after all is not with providing an exact factual record of physical conditions) but should instead turn to various of the other types of primary sources already mentioned: government papers, statistical series, company records, trade union archives, private correspondence, or various forms of archaeological remains. A painting or etching (or other form of visual art) *may* provide reliable information on what a particular environment looked like at a particular time – much of our knowledge of what seventeenth century London looked like, for instance, is derived in this way. But the historian must always remember that the painter may have been affected by prevailing stylistic conventions, or by his own artistic purposes, so that the painting is very far from being an exact factual record.

What the historian can usefully derive from imaginative literature is an insight into social *attitudes*, particularly attitudes towards that most subtle but important topic, *social status and social class,* and also attitudes towards matters of *belief* and *prejudice* (is the monarchy felt to be divine, is travelling on Sunday held to be sinful, etc.).

To gain this insight, the historian will, of course, have to saturate himself in the literature of the period: it is not good enough to lift a couple of easy quotations out of one or two novels, which may in fact turn out to be highly unrepresentative. Something of this perception, too, may be derived from visual art. It is, for instance, very striking that mediaeval artists tended to present peasants and craftsmen as if smaller in physical size than kings and great lords.

The formal *style* in which a painting or novel is conceived is a matter of great interest to the historian. For example a great deal can be learned about *changing attitudes* and *modes* of thought and expression, as between the mediaeval, the early Renaissance, and the high Renaissance periods from a study of the relevant art and architecture (see Dickens, especially pp. 108–13); or between the eighteenth and early nineteenth centuries, by comparing the formal, learned style of Reynolds with the fresher, more direct style of Constable, which suggests something of the 'individualism' of the age of 'the Romantic Revival'.

In looking at paintings in this way, the historian will also be concerned with the reception given to them by contemporaries. We learn much about early nineteenth century taste from knowing that Constable never achieved fashionable success, whereas his contemporary, Turner, who was in some ways an even greater innovator, had an immense reputation at the time.

A value to the historian provided by both art and literature is that they may suggest to him *questions* which he *ought to follow up* in other types of source. If he finds a statement or a description in a novel or a poem, or some piece of illustration in a painting, which does not seem to him to accord with the generally accepted picture of the age which he is studying, he will not immediately decide that this generally accepted picture must be overthrown. But on the other hand he will at least try to check from his other sources whether in fact there is any validity in the discrepancy which he has detected in his literary or artistic source.

Figure 21 Louis Le Nain, 1593–1648 Repas de paysans, Louvre MI 1088 (Peasants at supper) *(Photograph by courtesy of Musées Nationaux, Paris).*

Figure 22 Louis Le Nain, 1593–1648 Le retour de baptême Louvre, RF 1941–20 *(Return from christening) (Photograph by courtesy of Musées Nationaux, Paris).*

What conclusions might you draw about the life style, eating, drinking habits of the French peasantry in the seventeenth century?

Changing attitudes and modes of expression in eighteenth century and early nineteenth century paintings

Figure 23   Sir Joshua Reynolds Lady Cockburn and her children, *1773 (National Gallery, London).*

Figure 24   Richard Wilson Holt Ridge on the River Dee, c. 1762 *(National Gallery, London).*

Figure 25   John Constable Weymouth Bay, *1816–17 (National Gallery, London).*

Figure 26 John Constable
Salisbury Cathedral, *1820s*
(National Gallery, London).

Figure 27 J. M. W. Turner
Calais Pier, *1803 (National*
Gallery, London).

Figure 28 J. M. W. Turner
Hero and Leander, *1837*
(National Gallery, London).

Figure 29 J. M. W. Turner
The fighting 'Téméraire'
tugged to her last berth to
be broken up *(National*
Gallery, London).

The great danger which must always be guarded against in handling art and literature in historical study is that of presenting a too simple notion of art and literature 'reflecting' a particular age. More will be said about this later. But you might for the moment ponder over the danger that this notion that art and literature 'reflect' a particular age can simply degenerate into a circular argument. First of all the age is defined, say, the 'Elizabethan Age' or the 'Victorian Age': certain characteristics are attributed to these ages, most of them in fact drawn anyway from the art and literature of the age; then the art and literature are studied more systematically, when, lo and behold, the characteristics which have already been predetermined in the mind of the writer are discovered in the art and literature, and said to reflect their particular age.

This is by the way of being a warning, not an absolute embargo. Of course there is a very real relationship between the historical and social context and the art and literature of any particular age and society, and it is one of the tasks of the historian to explore this relationship. But you must always be on your guard against any simple use of art and literature as a 'mirror of the age' or as revealing 'the climate of the age' or whatever other question-begging cliché you care to use.

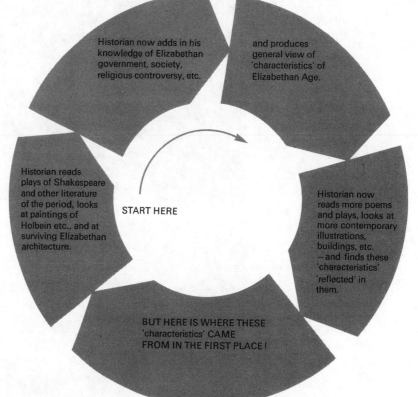

Historian now adds in his knowledge of Elizabethan government, society, religious controversy, etc.

and produces general view of 'characteristics' of Elizabethan Age.

Historian reads plays of Shakespeare and other literature of the period, looks at paintings of Holbein etc., and at surviving Elizabethan architecture.

START HERE

Historian now reads more poems and plays, looks at more contemporary illustrations, buildings, etc. – and finds these 'characteristics' 'reflected' in them.

BUT HERE IS WHERE THESE 'characteristics' CAME FROM IN THE FIRST PLACE!

The circular argument about art and literature 'reflecting' the age!

When you come to read *A Midsummer Night's Dream* and *Jane Eyre* you will find much fruitful interaction between historical and literary study, and that is what we want to encourage above all – but do try to keep the obvious dangers in mind.

Let us look in more detail at the poem, play, romance, novel, or short story as a historical primary source. There are three fundamental questions to which the historian must know the answers before he can make any use at all of this kind of source:

1 When was it written?

2 What period of time is it *written about*?

3 Did the author himself have first-hand experience of the events and circumstances he is purporting to describe?

One might perhaps qualify the third question by saying that if the author is drawing upon childhood memory, or perhaps even upon recollections of earlier times passed on to him by his family (though this is obviously more dubious) then the historian might be prepared to place a certain credence upon these memories and recollections even if they could not possibly be based on the author's own first-hand experience.

It is important, then, to get the dates right – both the date of writing, and the dates of the subject matter that the author is writing about. As we shall see there is a good deal of learned controversy about the exact dating of many of Shakespeare's works. Let me, however, take one rather striking example of potential misdating from the industrialization period.

This arises from the famous description of the poor-house in Charles Dickens's *Oliver Twist*. It is too often assumed that the description is of the grim new poor-houses built in accordance with the new Poor Law of 1834. Now, although the description was written in 1837, we know that practically none of the new poor-houses had in fact been built by this time; the description in *Oliver Twist*, therefore, really refers to the older kind of poor-house in existence before the new Poor Law of 1834. So you see how important it can be to get our dates sorted out.

For my exercise on this point I am going to stay with the industrialization period, keeping off the Renaissance for the time being.

EXERCISE

Turn to your collection of Supplementary Texts and carefully read the first three paragraphs from the extract of Mrs Gaskell's novel *Mary Barton* (document C3) quoted there. Read also the editor's introduction to this extract, then answer the following questions.

1 What dates are relevant to the historian in using this passage as a primary source?

2 Would those dates in themselves suggest that the passage is reliable or unreliable as a primary source? Answer YES or NO, and briefly give your reasons.

3 From these three paragraphs the historian might draw any or all of the following conclusions. Which of these conclusions (lettered from A to H) do you think most sensible and reasonable and which the least reasonable? Indicate your answer by placing the statements A to H in order from 1 to 8.

A That working-men in the late 1830s lived mainly on tea, sugar, butter, and flour; and they lived mainly in crowded garrets or damp cellars.

B That in early Victorian England there was an accepted distinction between working-men, often described simply as 'operatives', on the one side, and the upper class on the other.

C That a great working-class petition to Parliament was drawn up in the spring of 1839.

D That because of their sufferings the poor turned to 'rabid politics'.

E That the causes of the starvation and destitution are so complicated that it is practically impossible to explain them.

F That destitution affected thousands upon thousands of the population in the years 1839, 1840 and 1841.

G That in these years there was a 'feeling of alienation between different classes of society'.

H That to one novelist writing in 1848 (identified in the introduction to the extract as liberal and middle-class – you will have to take this on trust) one of the major characteristics of the period was the privation suffered by working-men.

SPECIMEN ANSWERS

1 The date of publication of the novel, 1848, and the period with which the novel is concerned, 1839–41.

2 Yes. 1848 is near enough in time to 1839–41 for it to seem reasonable that the author did in fact have some kind of direct experience of the events referred to.

3   1 – H
     2 – B
     3 – G
     4 – A
     5 – F
     6 – E
     7 – D
     8 – C

DISCUSSION

H is the most cautious conclusion, simply reporting directly upon the *opinions* expressed by the author, but not placing any credence upon the purported facts given by her. (We need other sources, of course, to establish the social class and political opinions which Mrs Gaskell represents.) In fact this is a rather important historical conclusion; writers of this sort did on the whole tend to emphasize the adverse effect on the mass of the people of industrialization, and this attitude itself has become very much a part of history.

B is just the sort of thing one would expect to derive from a novel. This really is *unwitting testimony*; Mrs Gaskell is not deliberately trying to make a point. It clearly comes naturally to her to use the sort of phrases quoted; and this in itself brings out very clearly the sort of class attitudes which operated in her day.

G Here the author is perhaps trying to make a more definite point; but nonetheless it is in this subtle area of class relations that one most depends on the evidence of creative literature.

A Here we have fairly factual information about eating and living conditions. It is the sort of information the historian would prefer to check against other, possibly more reliable, sources.

F Much the same is true of F. Mrs Gaskell's statistics are extremely vague, and the historian would much prefer to have some precise figures about destitution, standards of living and so on. But nonetheless, as was said of H, it is significant that so many novelists were quite clear about the existence of this destitution; and since concrete statistics are very hard to come by for this period, the historian is quite glad at least to have this preliminary guide to what conditions may have been like at this time.

E is really an expression of opinion on the part of the novelist. It is interesting to the historian that liberal writers like Mrs Gaskell did think that the causes of deprivation were 'next to impossible to understand thoroughly'. But of course the historian would not accept that in reality the causes are inexplicable; indeed he might well have many theories of his own, based on his study of economic and other evidence, of what had brought about this desperate situation.

D is another clear expression of opinion on the part of the author. 'Rabid politics' is a rather emotional phrase showing, incidentally, that although the middle-class Mrs Gaskell had sympathy with the poor in their sufferings, she had much less sympathy for their attempts to turn to political action. If the historian's conclusions had been phrased in the indirect way in which H was phrased, then, of course, this would be one of the most important conclusions.

C concerns a straightforward matter of political fact. But it is a golden rule that the historian does not depend for such basic factual information on works of literature. There are many much better sources which he could turn to. (Of course it may well be true that in certain societies certain novels provide more *reliable* information than other, government-controlled sources; but even here the novel is unlikely to be reliable for absolutely precise factual information – that is not the novelist's business.)

Now the novel you will actually be studying in the course is Charlotte Brontë's *Jane Eyre*.

EXERCISE

What again are the three basic questions the historian would ask before using this as a source? Do you have any idea, at this stage, of any of the answers?

Figures 30 (a) and (b)   Women in World War I

Figures 31 (a) and (b)   Women in World War II

Visual evidence: the changing or the unchanging role of women in the twentieth century. Reflect on this sort of evidence along with the evidence on the role of women in *Jane Eyre*

SPECIMEN ANSWER

1 *When was it written?* You can see at a glance that it was *published* in 1847. Once you have got to grips with your study of the book you will find out that, as it would be reasonable to guess anyway, it was *written* during the previous year, 1846.

2 *What period of time was it written about?* The novel is described on the title page as 'an autobiography', and we know that Charlotte Brontë was born in 1816. We know that there was a real orphans' school, Cowan Bridge, which Charlotte Brontë attended in the mid-1820s, and which is very like Lowood in the novel. But there are inconsistencies – a reference to Sir Walter Scott's *Marmion* would seem to push the novel further back in time. The fact is, we cannot expect absolutely precise dating in a novel; but for giving us insight into certain attitudes held in the early nineteenth century, *Jane Eyre* serves very well.

3 *Did the author herself have first-hand experience of the events and circumstances she is purporting to describe?* For Lowood, for experiences as a governess, for encounters with clergymen, the answer is very definitely yes; as also for what, in general, it was like to be a young woman in early nineteenth century society.

This is not the place to look at *Jane Eyre* in detail. Let me just remark here that what particularly interests *me* as a historian are the assumptions about class, about religion, and about the role and status of women. I am also struck by the concern with, and concepts of, personal beauty – but that begins to take us beyond mere history.

Let it finally be repeated that the purpose of imaginative literature is not to provide information for the historian. The important questions to be asked concern the aesthetic, creative side of the work being studied. On the other hand, as we have seen, such works can have immense value for the historian as *unwitting testimony*.

6 THE IMPERFECT AND FRAGMENTARY NATURE OF HISTORICAL SOURCES

If you have followed the material presented in this unit you should now be aware that the historian's task is by no means an easy one. The difficulties we have discussed could be summarized under two headings: (1) the immense range and variety of the sources which the historian must be prepared to make use of; and (2) the complicated critical techniques which he has to bring to bear on these sources once he has found them. But this does not really complete the picture. You may feel that once the sources have been discovered, once authenticity has been established, and once the various biases have been allowed for and the various technical problems resolved, then it is fairly plain sailing towards producing a reasonable reconstruction of whatever aspect of the past the particular historian is interested in; but this is not necessarily so, since however dedicated and skilful the historian, nothing can compensate for the fact that most of the sources bequeathed to us by past ages are extremely fragmentary and imperfect. For certain well-documented periods it is possible to provide a clear outline of events: but you should always beware of the historian who tries to ride roughshod over the difficulties of his subject, presenting glib interpretations without even attempting to discuss the nature of his evidence.

In the next unit I shall turn specifically to the question of controversy in historical writing, that is, the manner in which disagreement arises among the most distinguished and hard-working historians over their interpretations of past events. We have already noted possible reasons for this, particularly the unavoidable subjective element in history. But it must be stressed that even if by some undesirable miracle the subjective element could be wished away, historians would still find themselves in disagreement. Even if their methods could become much more purely scientific, the very fact that the evidence is so imperfect and so fragmentary would still leave much scope for controversy.

Let us look at some of the more obvious ways in which primary source material is fragmentary and imperfect. First of all, taking our archaeological and other kinds of physical evidence, it is obvious that much of it, when discovered, is in very bad condition indeed.

It is very seldom indeed that an archaeological dig uncovers complete, undamaged relics of past ages. And even when the relics are in a perfect condition, remember that these physical remains only provide a few tiny clues to the total picture of what life was like, and what events were taking place, in that bygone age. This is the place to repeat the warning against those popular accounts which dogmatically describe, in picturesque detail, exactly what life was like in some remote age; remember that such descriptions must always be no more than *attempts* at reconstruction derived from very imperfect evidence. (This is not a counsel of despair: of course great scholars have done marvellous things with the most unpromising material – the point is for you to develop an *awareness* of what is involved.)

Archaeological sources are not the only ones to suffer from the depredations of time. Frequently charters and other written documents have survived in a form which renders them practically unreadable. Even where a document is complete, or relatively complete, there are still, as we noted in section 3, all kinds of problems of comprehending archaic languages or strange scripts and hieroglyphics. The historian faced with a text in ancient Sanskrit or even in mediaeval Latin or mediaeval French can never be absolutely sure that the meaning he has given to certain words is the same meaning understood by people of the time. For example, many of the more exaggerated claims which Victorian historians made on behalf of Magna Carta as being a basic charter of English liberties, establishing parliamentary government and trial by jury, were due to placing an unjustifiably modern interpretation on certain Latin phrases.

However much material the historian has at his disposal he will never find everything necessary for answering the particular questions he wishes to ask. We have already noted the value to the historian of *unwitting testimony*, which tends to exist independently of the overt purposes and biases of the writer of the document. On the other hand, by very definition, unwitting testimony means that the originator of it had completely different questions in mind from the ones which the historian would like to see answered. This is particularly true when the attempt is made to describe the social structure of a past society, or to determine standards of living, and so on. Men in past ages did not have our interest in these problems, and therefore they tended not to leave the sort of primary source material which would yield answers to them. This means that historians concerned with such problems have to deduce their interpretations in all kinds of indirect ways. For example (to take yet another instance from the industrialization period), one historian (Professor E. J. Hobsbawm) has tried to make up for the lack of direct statistical evidence on the general standard of living in Britain in the early nineteenth century by seeking to derive this *indirectly* from the sales of meat at the Smithfield meat market in London. Because he can say fairly definitely that sales of meat were not increasing when population definitely was increasing, he therefore argues that the standard of living cannot have been rising, and probably was falling. This is a perfectly reasonable inference to make, but clearly it is open to attack from other historians; and it was in fact attacked by Dr R. M. Hartwell, who has argued that the Smithfield figures are insufficient in themselves, that we need to know more about meat markets in other parts of the country, that we need to take into account imports from abroad, and that we must include the increased consumption of fish in our calculations. Taking all of these things into account, Dr Hartwell came to rather different conclusions from Professor Hobsbawm. Perhaps the argument never can be settled, since the direct evidence which would be necessary simply has not been preserved, or perhaps never existed: early nineteenth century governments did not have our own interest in compiling cost-of-living indices.

In discussing the imperfect nature of primary source material, it is worth distinguishing the special problems of (1) the historian of the middle ages, and (2) the historian of the modern world. Neither kind of historian will ever be able to get all the material he wants to answer particular questions. But while the mediaeval historian usually suffers from extreme fragmentation in his evidence, so that he frequently has to build up interpretations from only a handful of documents and a few pieces of non-traditional evidence (archaeology, place names, aerial photographs), the modern historian often finds that he has too much material. The Renaissance period we are interested in, of course, falls bang in the middle. It is during the Renaissance that the number of sources begins to multiply rapidly, and that they begin to be better preserved. Historians of the early Renaissance tend to share the problems of the historian of the middle ages; historians of the late Renaissance begin to share the problems of the modernist. Strictly speaking, the modern historian should consult every relevant and available source, just as any other historian should. But if you think for a moment of the way in which the written and printed word has proliferated in the last hundred years, resulting in documentary material pouring out by the ton, you will see that this may be a counsel of perfection. Often the modern historian has to devise special methods of *selectivity* in his use of source material. If he selects wrongly, then of course his interpretation of the evidence will be dubious; it will always be open to direct challenge from someone who has been more systematically through a wider range of sources. It is because of this increasing burden of source material in the modern era that the use of computers (principally for storing information, for making complicated statistical calculations, and for devising mathematically sound samples of the impossible mass of source material) has become so important. Nonetheless there is the curious paradox that increasing use of the telephone in the twentieth century has meant that for certain crucial decisions there is *no written (or any other) record at all*.

Whatever different problems historians in different areas encounter, there always comes a point when a historian has to *squeeze the last drop* of information out of the evidence. This is a good image, and worth remembering.

EXERCISE

Read these passages from historical works, both concerned with rather remote periods of London history; *A* with fourth-century Roman London, *B* with tenth- and eleventh-century Saxon London, Indicate which passage you think recognizes more realistically the fragmentary nature of historical sources.

Passage A

Across the Thames, a little further downstream than the present London Bridge, was a wooden bridge, wide enough to carry two streams of traffic, one leaving Londinium for the transriverine suburb, whose site now lies buried beneath the streets of Southwark, the other stream entering the city through the gate whose towers looked down upon the square-rigged ships moored at the long wharfs below.

Inside the walls the paved main streets of the city's centre were wide and straight and regular, the buildings that lined them solid and imposing. Although the labourers and the men who worked on the docks still lived in little huts like beehives or in wooden houses with thatched or shingle roofs, much of the Roman reconstruction that had followed the devastation of the city by Boadicea had been carried out in brick, stone and tile. Most buildings, their walls painted a dark red, their low-pitched roofs a lighter, salmon colour, were small and low; but there were others, it seems, four or even five storeys high with fountains playing in their courtyards and vines growing against their garden walls.

The Basilica, centre of commerce and government, which faced the traveller as he entered the city through the river gate, was a vast and impressive building on Cornhill, five hundred feet long, whose arcaded walls, lined inside with marble, were about seventy feet high; while the temple dedicated to the mysterious Mithras, the Persian god of light whose cult had been adopted by the Legions, was as graceful as any to be found in the western provinces of the Empire.

Passage B

The pre-Norman bridge of London is first mentioned, by chance, in a charter of the reign of the Saxon King Edgar (AD 959–75), in connection with a woman deliberately drowned as a witch for pin-sticking: *adrencte hir aet Lundenebridgce*. Other Saxon references to the bridge occur during the reigns of Ethelred II (978–1016) and his eldest son, Edmund Ironside (1016). The name of the former is specially closely connected with the bridge in several ways. In his fourth code of laws, which is concerned only with London (*De Institutis de Lundonie*), it is laid down that toll was to be paid for vessels coming to the bridge with fish: a halfpenny was due from a small ship and a penny from a larger one. During these two reigns the second wave of Viking invasion was at its height, and it is recorded in the *Anglo-Saxon Chronicle* under the year 1013 that when Swein Forkbeard, King of Denmark, who had marched from Winchester, was about to besiege London many of his men were drowned in the Thames 'because they kept not to the bridge'. Two years later, in 1015, there is a description of the bridge and of a fight for it in *St Olaf's Saga*, written down in the thirteenth century in praise of Olaf Haroldson, the Christian king of the Norwegians, who died in 1030 and was rapidly accepted as a saint. This stirring tale of the bridge is not recorded in the contemporary *Anglo-Saxon Chronicle* but its essential elements are probably true.

. . . Some years ago, at the turn of last century, several weapons and tools were found lying together in the alluvium of the former foreshore of the Thames not far from the north end of the late Norman bridge of London. The implements included battle axes, spearheads, a grappling iron, a woodman's axe and a pair of tongs. As they would seem to be part of the equipment of a Viking warship, and can be dated as not much later than AD 1000, it is probable that they are associated with the Viking attacks detailed above on the old Saxon timber bridge, the site of which will be considered later.

SPECIMEN ANSWER AND DISCUSSION

A's description of Roman London is just too smooth and self-confident, given that the main sources are archaeological. *B* recognizes much more openly the nature of the various types of source from which information can be squeezed.

Note that we are not concerned with the quality of these passages as *historical communication* (a vitally important aspect to be discussed in the next unit). Passage *B* certainly is too disjointed to rank as good historical writing. But that is not the point at issue here.

EXERCISE

Here are some photographs of fragmentary or difficult historical sources. Say what you think each is, comment on the difficulties in using it, and suggest what positive uses could be made of it by the historian.

Figure 32

Figure 33

Figure 34

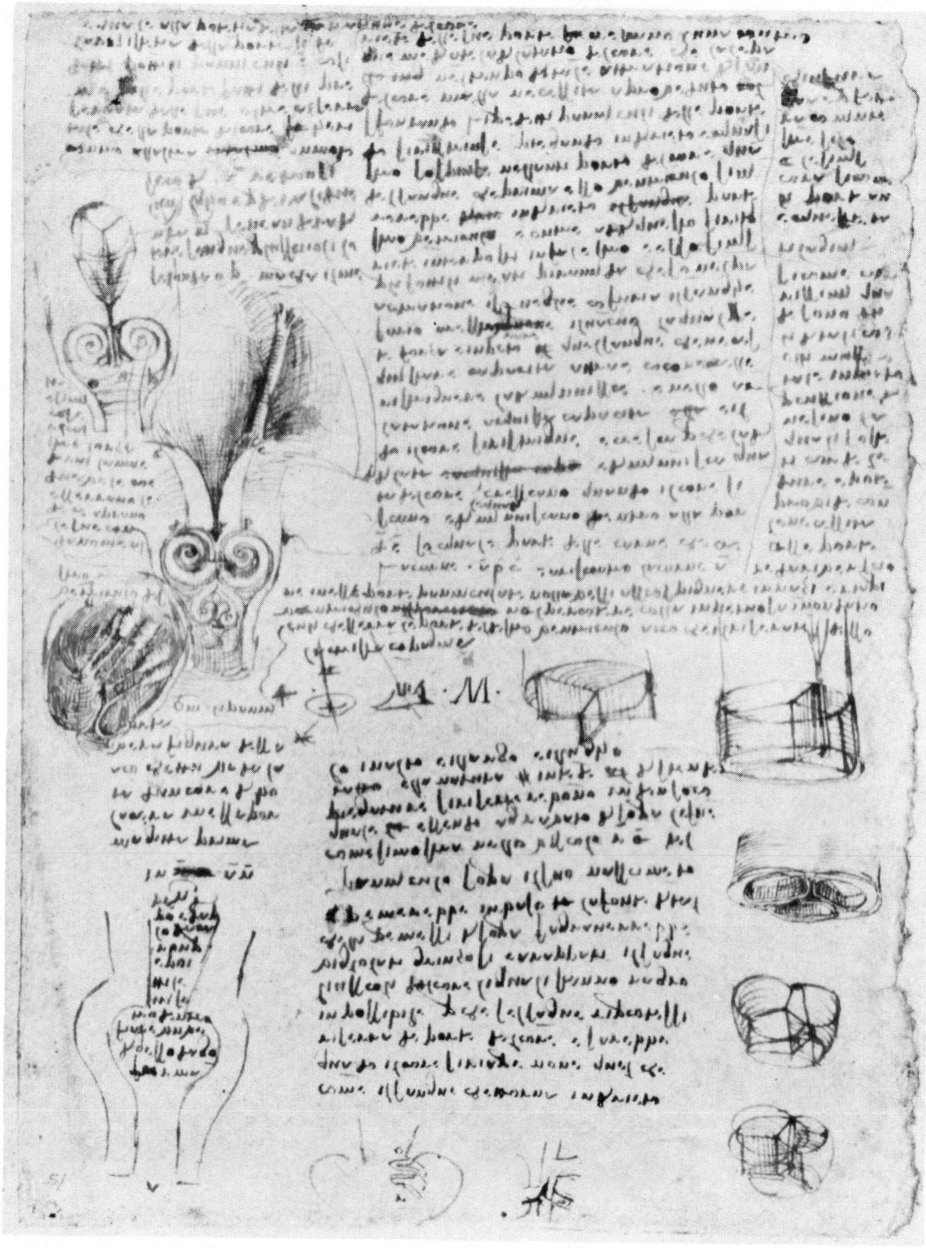

Figure 35

SPECIMEN ANSWERS

Figure 32 This is a pot or vessel, used probably for oil, or perhaps wine. Although we have only a part, there is enough to suggest the general shape and dimensions of the pot. Obviously before we can make much use of this source, we have to ask the usual questions: how did it come into existence, etc. For this sort of source, we would also need to know where it was found. Needless to say, I do not expect you to have any full answers to these questions, but I hope that your mind was beginning to grope in the right direction. Certainly, the pot must tell us something about the domestic lifestyle of the people who used it. I hope at least you got that relatively simple point. But, in fact, for the expert even this fragment of evidence can tell a great deal more. Archaeologists can attribute its origins to the East Mediterranean; since in fact it was found in London, in a layer of soil which archaeologists believe to have been deposited after the fifth century, this fragment can be taken as evidence that trade continued between the East Mediterranean and London after the fifth century.

Figure 33 This is not an easy one to make out. In fact it is the remains of a Roman ship. Again, even from these fragments, we can build up a picture of the entire ship. We can also, in the background to the left, discern the cargo of stone.

To tell more than this, the evidence has to be fitted in to the broader contexts in exactly the same way as with the fragment of pot.

Figure 34   What is immediately striking about this charter is its extreme brevity. You can see clearly what the original Anglo-Saxon looks like, and grasp immediately some of the problems of translation. Even in translation, there remain many of the sorts of technical problems we have already discussed. However, as a charter this is a document of record (it is in fact William the Conqueror's Charter to the City of London) and must therefore tell us something substantial and concrete.

Figure 35   Again, just by looking at this, you can see the problems of interpretation. These are in fact notes and sketches by one of the great figures of the Italian Renaissance, Leonardo Da Vinci. As you may know, he made these notes in 'mirror writing'. However, once the technique of interpreting them has been mastered, obviously they are an absolutely first class source for the ideas and thoughts of this very important Renaissance figure.

EXERCISE

Here now is an excerpt from one of the most important sources for twentieth-century British political history. It is an extract from the Cabinet Minutes in August 1931, at the time of the great crisis which destroyed the second Labour government. The Labour government is meeting for the last time under the Prime Ministership of Ramsay MacDonald. Here we have a vital source for events which have been a matter of controversy ever since. Yet, I want you to comment on the imperfections and inadequacies of this source from the point of view of a historian writing an account of the crisis.

> In conclusion, the Prime Minister said that it must be admitted that the proposals as a whole, represented the negation of everything that the Labour Party stood for, and yet he was absolutely satisfied that it was necessary, in the national interests, to implement them if the country was to be secure. He then pointed out that, if on this question there were any important resignations, the Government as a whole must resign.
>
> Each member then expressed views on the proposed ten per cent cut in unemployment benefits.
>
> In the course of these expressions of view, indications were given that, while a majority of the Cabinet favoured the inclusion in the economy proposals of the ten per cent reduction in unemployment insurance benefit, the adoption of this as part and parcel of the scheme would involve the resignation of certain Ministers from the Government.

Figure 36   Ramsay MacDonald and National Government in the garden of No. 10 Downing Street, August 1931 (Radio Times Hulton Picture Library).

97

SPECIMEN ANSWER

As a formal Cabinet record, the minutes fail to give us much of the detailed information we really need. We learn that a *minority* (an important point, incidentally, long a subject of dispute) were opposed to the proposed cuts; but we do not learn who they were, or what arguments they put forward.

7 COMMUNICATION

The practice of history involves four basic activities.

1   The historian must go out and find his source materials.

2   He must bring to bear on them the critical techniques I have just been discussing, and the knowledge he already has of the period and topic he is studying.

3   Out of this interaction he must produce an *interpretation*, his version of events and relationships between events, including, as relevant, his explanation of *why* people did what they did.

4   Finally, he must *communicate* this interpretation to his audience.

As a student you too will go through these activities, though of course your sources will (I hope!) not be too hard to find, and your interpretations will not quite be of the same character as those of a historical scholar. But if you are to be a good student of history, and, indeed, of the humanities, you must be able to communicate.

Even if the professional historian has made marvellous new discoveries in primary source material which no one else has ever seen, he has not completed his job if these discoveries remain buried in his own head, and are never communicated to anyone else. The audience to which the historian communicates may be small (other specialist historians) or large (the entire reading public); but whatever audience he is communicating with, the historian must present his findings in a proper and acceptable fashion.

The communication will be in the form of a book, or article, or perhaps a lecture or a radio talk. Once written, such books, articles etc. form what we have already described as secondary sources. Put in a different way, the final task of the historian can be described as the conversion of the 'raw material' of the primary sources into the finished product, the secondary source – still a 'source' in the sense that this finished product will be the main source of information for students and the general reader, people who do not have the time or the ability to search all the primary sources every time they want a particular bit of historical information.

Later in this course you will have to present your findings, in history, in literature, etc., and in inter-disciplinary work in the form of a properly written essay. If we now study the way in which the historian turns primary sources into properly written history this should both contribute to your understanding of the nature of history as a discipline, and to your skill in writing essays in all of your humanities subjects.

Let us start again with the vital distinction between primary and secondary sources. For this exercise you will again need your Supplementary Texts.

EXERCISE

Some of the passages listed below are from primary, some from secondary sources. When you have studied them indicate which are primary and which secondary, and briefly note down reasons for your decision. Finally discuss any connections you detect between the various passages.

> *Passage A*
> No free man shall be seized or imprisoned, or stripped of his rights or possessions, or outlawed or exiled, or deprived of his standing in any other way, nor will we proceed with force against him, or send others to do so, except by the lawful judgement of his equals or by the law of the land.

Passage B
Then arose new architects, and they, after the manner of their barbarous nations, erected the buildings in that style which we now call Gothic, and raising edifices that, to us moderns, are rather to the discredit than glory of the builders, until at a later period there appeared better artists, who returned, in some measure, to the purer style of the antique; and this may be seen in most of the old (but not antique) churches throughout Italy, which were built in the manner just alluded to by these last-named artists. . . .

It was only by slow degrees that those who came after, being aided in some places by the subtlety of the air around them, could begin to raise themselves from these depths; when, towards 1250, Heaven, moved to pity by the noble spirits which the Tuscan soil was producing every day, restored them to their primitive conditions. It is true that those who lived in the times succeeding the ruin of Rome, had seen remnants of arches, colossi, statues, pillars, storied columns, and other works of art, not wholly destroyed by the fires and other devastations; yet they had not known how to avail themselves of this aid, nor had they derived any benefit from it, until the times specified above.

Passage C
In the character of these States, whether republics or despotisms, lies, not the only, but the chief reason for the early development of the Italian into modern man. It is this that made it inevitable that he should be the first-born among the sons of modern Europe.

In the Middle Ages both sides of human consciousness – that which was turned within and that which was turned without – lay as though dreaming or half awake beneath a common veil. The veil was woven of faith, illusion, and childish pre-possession, through which the world and history were seen clad in strange hues. Man was conscious of himself only as a member of a race, people, party, family, or corporation – only through some general category. It is in Italy that this veil dissolved first; there arose an *objective* treatment and consideration of the State and of all the things of this world, and at the same time the *subjective* side asserted itself with corresponding emphasis. Man became a spiritual *individual*, and recognized himself as such. In the same way the Greek had once distinguished himself from the barbarian, and the Arab had felt himself an individual at a time when other Asiatics knew themselves only as members of a race. It will not be difficult to show that this result was due above all to the political circumstances of Italy.

From Jacob Burckhardt, *The Civilization of the Renaissance in Italy*, originally published in 1860.

Passage D
To obtain the general consent of the realm for the assessment of an 'aid' – except in three cases specified above – or a 'scutage', we will cause the archbishops, bishops, abbots, earls, and greater barons to be summoned individually by letter. To those who hold lands directly of us we will cause a general summons to be issued, through the sheriffs and other officials, to come together on a fixed day (of which at least forty days notice shall be given) and at a fixed place.

Passage E
To no one will we sell, to no one deny or delay right or justice.

Passage F
Where was the painter's art till Giotto tardily restored it? A caricature of human delineation! Sculpture and architecture, for long years sunk to the merest travesty of art, are only today in process of rescue from obscurity; only now are they being brought to a new pitch of perfection by men of genius and eludition. Of letters and liberal studies at large it were best to be silent altogether. For these, the real guides to distinction in all the arts, the solid foundation of all civilisation, have been lost to mankind for eight hundred years and more. It is but in our own day that men dare boast that they see the dawn of better things. For example, we owe it to our Leonardo Bruni that Latin, so long a by-word for its uncouthness, has begun to shine forth in its ancient purity, its beauty, its majestic rhythm. Now, indeed, may every thoughtful spirit thank God that it has been permitted to him to be born in this new age, so full of hope and promise, which already rejoices

in a greater array of nobly-gifted souls than the world has seen in the thousand years that have preceded it.

Passage G
Defined with varying chronological limits, the age of the Renaissance has been perhaps more than any other subjected to the search for a single common denominator, the unique and fundamental change whose effects could be perceived in every department of human activity. Burckhardt's famous generalisations opened new horizons and had a measurable effect on the whole subsequent course of historical thinking, but nearly a century and many thousands of pages later we can think of many instances where the well-known formula has been statistically applied and where it has obstructed rather than advanced our understanding of particular phenomena.

Passage H
. . . Magna Carta has come to be regarded by Englishmen, and by all those who adopted English laws, as their chief constitutional defence against arbitrary or unjust rule. Its two most famous clauses express and give warranty to some of the Englishman's most deeply held political beliefs. In these and other clauses, seventeenth-century lawyers were to find a basis for such fundamental English privileges and rights as trial by jury, Habeas Corpus, equality before the law, freedom from arbitrary arrest, and parliamentary control of taxation.

SPECIMEN ANSWER

From the direct, positive phrasing, together with the technical, and in some cases archaic, terminology, it should be clear that *A*, *D* and *E* are all from a primary source, a charter or other document of record. They are in fact all from Magna Carta.

From the phrasing of the documents (e.g. the use of 'modern' and 'our' for the Renaissance period) it should be clear that *B* and *F* are also primary documents expressing a contemporary view about the nature of the Renaissance which the writers believed to be taking place around them.

Since *C* was published in 1860, yet is about the Renaissance period, it is clearly a secondary source. Burckhardt is in fact one of the first great interpreters of the Renaissance. Clearly *G* (in fact from *The World of Humanism* by Myron P. Gilmore) is from a later secondary source which is taking Burckhardt's interpretation as a kind of jumping off point.

H is clearly a historian's interpretation of Magna Carta, a secondary source.

As primary sources, *B* and *F* are closely linked together as presenting a very similar contemporary view of the nature of the Renaissance. Burckhardt's interpretation of the Renaissance (*C*) obviously draws in part on documents such as these, and *G* is in turn linked to all of these.

A, *D* and *E* are all in fact from Magna Carta. *H*, which, obviously, is linked to them, is a good example of the interpreting historian at work: he includes not just information drawn from the clauses of Magna Carta, but a statement about English constitutional attitudes (first sentence) which is necessarily based on very wide reading; and the last sentence contains information drawn from legal cases and the writings and speeches of lawyers in the seventeenth century.

EXERCISE

You have been researching on the somewhat shadowy Elizabethan figure Sir Christopher Bentlowe (just in case you're bothered, he's a complete invention, purely for the purposes of this exercise). You have discovered.

1   A hitherto unknown play *The Virgin King* which you know was first performed in 1589. In certain aspects it seems almost to go beyond the contemporary Shakespeare in quality, and it has original characteristics which

in conjunction with some external evidence confirms your view that it was written by Bentlowe.

2 Some poems of an explicit homosexual character which, though you cannot date them, you can firmly attribute to Bentlowe.

3 Certain household accounts showing that over a fifteen-year period Bentlowe consumed fifteen gallons of sack (sherry) a week.

4 Privy Council records of 1591 which show that Bentlowe, as a member of the Privy Council, had ambitious ideas for a new Poor Law.

5 A religious tract of 1592 attacking Bentlowe for licentiousness and ungodliness.

6 Memoirs of William Cecil, Lord Burghley, principal adviser of the Queen, referring to Sir Christopher Bentlowe, in 1588, as a very able counsellor and statesman.

7 Contemporary accounts of Bentlowe's death in a tavern brawl in 1595.

8 Persistent fragments of information 1588–95 showing Bentlowe's interest in the social problems of vagrancy and the deserving poor.

9 Parish records indicating Bentlowe's birth in 1555, as the son of a small tradesman.

10 By comparing the parts of the Poor Law of 1598 dealing with the deserving poor with Bentlowe's ideas, you can see very marked similarities.

In your notebook, *communicate* this information in the form of a brief piece of historical writing such as might appear in a secondary source.

SPECIMEN ANSWER

Now here are three different attempts which, as I hope you will see at once, are of very different levels of attainment.

Passage A Bentlowe wrote a play, *The Virgin King*, first performed in 1589, which is Shakespearean in quality. He also wrote poems (date uncertain) of an explicitly homosexual character. His household accounts suggest that he was a heavy drinker. In 1591, as a Privy Counsellor, he had ambitious ideas for a new Poor Law. He was attacked as licentious and ungodly in 1593 though regarded very highly as a statesman five years earlier. He died in a tavern brawl in 1595. He seems to have been consistently interested in Poor Law problems. He was born in 1555 in relatively humble circumstances, and must have risen in the world to receive his knighthood in or before 1588. He seems to have influenced the Poor Law of 1598.

Passage B Bentlowe was born in 1555, the son of a small tradesman. By 1588 he had achieved some reputation as a statesman, and a knighthood or baronetcy. He was also a poet and playwright and the following year his great play *The Virgin King* was produced. In 1591 he presented the Privy Council with ambitious ideas for Poor Law reform. He was attacked as 'licentious and ungodly' and he seems to have been both a drunkard and a homosexual. He continued his interest in the Poor Law. He was killed in a tavern brawl in 1595. The Poor Law of 1598 shows signs of his influence.

Passage C Born in 1555 in relatively humble circumstances, Christopher Bentlowe rose rapidly in the world becoming a Privy Counsellor and a knight (or baronet) by 1588, when he earned the praises of William Cecil. In 1591 he put forward ambitious ideas for a new Poor Law, a question which had preoccupied him, and continued to preoccupy him, for several years: some of these ideas seem to have influenced the Poor Law eventually enacted in 1598. Bentlowe was also a poet and playwright, and in 1589 his masterpiece *The Virgin King*, which in some respects rivals, or even outdistances, Shakespeare, was produced for the first time. Yet he died an obscure death in a tavern brawl in 1595. Some clues to his dramatic rise and fall may lie in his private life: he was attacked as licentious and ungodly and there is evidence that he was both a heavy drinker and a homosexual.

DISCUSSION

C is obviously the best of these three passages: it is clear, orderly, and it reads smoothly. B is not so good, though it is preferable to A which is very bad as a piece of communication. The faults of presentation in A and B will be discussed in Unit 5, when we turn to form and structure in historical writing.

Looking closely at C you will note that even in so short a piece of historical writing as this it is practically impossible (and probably not desirable) simply to 'report the facts'. The phrase 'some clues . . . may lie in his private life' is a cautious one, but it does show the introduction of an element of *interpretation*. Meantime check your own answer to be sure that it corresponds more closely to C than to A.

It may be, though, that you have produced a version which differs quite a lot from C, yet is equally good as *communication*. In fact there can be no absolute and final way of setting down even the limited information you have discovered about Bentlowe. This is one of the problems in assessing how good you are at history (or indeed how good a professional historian is): there can be no absolute, one hundred per cent guide as to how you should present your material. But the point to remember is that the material must be communicated: in general it is true to say that some ways are better than others for making sure that information is effectively communicated.

History must above all be firmly grounded in the sources; but a person who does not present his material in good English has failed to complete his tasks as a historian. It is always worth remembering that if your presentation is bad, the reader may not be able to follow your facts, however laboriously discovered, or your ideas, however brilliant.

Unit 4 ends here. If you are ahead of time, get on with the next unit. Remember that at the end of Unit 5, you also have to do a tutor-marked assignment.

UNIT 5 THE WRITING OF HISTORY

CONTENTS

OBJECTIVES OF EACH SECTION

Section 1   The Basic Elements of Form and Structure in Historical Writing
You must yourself, when writing any sort of history, know how to communicate in the clearest and best way.

Section 2   Selection in Historical Writing
You must know what to leave out, when you are writing any kind of history.

Section 3   Narrative, Analysis and Description
To help you in your own writing, and to help you in reading works by other historians, you should be able to break historical writing down into its three central elements, narrative, analysis and description.

Section 4   Planning a History Essay
You should develop the skill of planning your essays so that they communicate as clearly as possible, and you should be aware of how far this skill is common to writing all types of essays, and how far there are special problems in planning a history essay.

Section 5   Quotations, Footnotes and Bibliographies
You should understand why such things as footnotes, bibliographies, and so on are essential to good historical writing, even if they are not necessary in your own essays.

Section 6   Types of Historical Communication
You should be able to distinguish between the different levels of historical writing (e.g. PhD thesis, text book, popular history); and be able to criticize a work on each level on its own merits.

Section 7   Periodization and Historical Semantics
You should understand why in order to write history we have to chop the past up into 'periods', and you should be aware of the dangers of doing this. You should also know how to use, and how not to use, some of the more obvious difficult words in history, such as *feudalism, revolution, capitalism*, etc.

Section 8   Controversy in Historical Writing
You should appreciate that historians don't just disagree with each other for the hell of it, and you should be able to explain the manner in which controversy among historians may further historical discovery.

Section 9   History and the Other Humanities
You should be able to discuss critically potentially fruitful areas of overlap between history and the other humanities, and, in a very preliminary way, you should be aware of how philosophers and historians deal with the question of 'explanation' in history.

Section 10   Conclusion: Evaluating History and Historians
You should now have a better basis for assessing historical writing – your own essays, books by professional historians and also films, television and radio programmes, and popular works dealing with history.

1 THE BASIC ELEMENTS OF FORM AND STRUCTURE IN HISTORICAL WRITING

Passages *A* and *B* in the last exercise in Unit 4 (p. 102) do not communicate a very clear statement about Bentlowe because they are badly organized, they lack form. *A* is particularly weak because it simply sets down the pieces of information about Bentlowe as they turned up, without any attempt to place them in logical sequence. *B* is rather better because it has at least arranged the information in chronological sequence: that is, beginning with his birth and working through the years till his death and his posthumous influence in the Poor Law of 1598. The trouble here is that each fact – important and unimportant – is given equal weight; and there is no attempt to establish any meaningful relationship between different facts. As far as this passage is concerned, his ideas for Poor Law reform might be directly related to his licentiousness and ungodliness.

Of course, form or organization is required in any piece of writing, not just historical writing. The point is that facts and ideas thrown together in any kind of slap-dash sequence simply will not communicate themselves to someone else; indeed, disorderly presentation usually suggests that the writer himself is not completely clear in his own mind. To grasp something quickly and firmly, the human mind demands orderliness: it is fairly easy to grasp the contents of a bookshelf in which the books are arranged systematically by subject; it is much less easy to do so when the books are crammed in any old how, or even when (as has been known) they are arranged in accordance with the colour of their binding.

In writing, the basic purpose of organization is to get the emphasis right, to direct the reader away from less important matter, while making sure that he has grasped the really important information.

The difference between the Bentlowe passage *C* and passages *A* and *B* lies in the effort which has gone into *C* to get the emphasis right. In the first sentence, the date of birth is treated rather as incidental, the real weight falling on the positive point that from humble origins Bentlowe rose rapidly in the world. From there, we pass in the next two sentences to the two central points about Bentlowe: his contribution to the Elizabethan Poor Law, and his contribution to Elizabethan drama. But, almost in the same breath as it were, the 'yet' sentence adds on the essential tragedy of his life – he achieved nothing more and died an obscure death. Lastly, with slightly less emphasis, we come to the details of his private life, which through a simple piece of interpretation by the historian are deliberately presented as a possible explanation of his dramatic rise and fall.

Bentlowe is an invention and not altogether a likely figure for Elizabethan England; and even passage *C* is rather too simplified to be really like any piece of history you would be likely to encounter in a book, or would be likely to write yourself in an essay. Here therefore is a passage taken from a real book. (*History of the Elizabethan Stage*, by E. K. Chambers.)

EXERCISE

1   Say in a few lines what is wrong with this passage.

2   Rewrite it so that it communicates more clearly.

> The great spectacles of [Elizabeth's] reign were liturgies, undertaken by her gallants, or by the nobles whose country houses she visited in the course of her annual progresses. The most famous of all, the 'Princely Pleasure of Kenilworth' in 1575, was at the expense of Dudley, to whom the ancient royal castle had long been alienated. Gradually, no doubt, the financial stringency was relaxed. Camden notes a growing tendency to luxury about 1574; others trace the change to the coming of the Duke of Alençon in 1581. Elizabeth had found the way to evoke a national spirit, and at the same time

107

to fill her coffers, by the encouragement of piratical enterprise, and the sumptuous entertainments prepared for the welcome of Monsieur were paid for out of the spoils brought back by Drake in the *Golden Hind*. The Alençon negotiations, whether seriously intended or not, represent Elizabeth's last dalliance with the idea of matrimony. They gave way to that historic part of unapproachable virginity, whereby an elderly Cynthia, without complete loss of dignity, was enabled to the end to maintain a sentimental claim upon the attentions, and the purses of her youthful servants. The strenuous years, which led up to the final triumph over the Armada in 1588, spared but little room for revels and for progresses. They left Elizabeth an old woman. But with the removal of the strain, the spirit of gaiety awoke.[1]

Figure 1   George Gower Queen Elizabeth I, *Armada portrait, c.* 1588 (By kind permission of the Marquess of Tavistock and the Trustees of the Bedford Estates, Woburn Abbey).

SPECIMEN ANSWER

1   What is wrong with this passage is that it is totally disorganized. Facts and ideas tumble out in a very disorderly way. Thus although there is obviously a good deal of valuable information contained in the passage, it is impossible to grasp it since the presentation is so bad.

Clearly the author has done what you may often be tempted to do in writing an essay (but, with this awful example in front of you, you should avoid at all costs): he has simply served up his notes as they stand, without any attempt to organize them (that is to say, give them a structure) in a manner which will communicate readily with someone else. There is no point in the author (or you, or anyone) saying that his facts are right, his ideas illuminating, if it is practically impossible for anyone else to discover what his facts and ideas are.

2   The passage rewritten:
As rich men in classical Athens paid for the tragedies and comedies, so the great spectacles of Elizabeth's reign were paid for by her gallants, or by the

[1]The passage is also quoted by Barzun and Graff *The Modern Researcher* (first edition 1957), a book which is discussed in *The Nature of History*, pp. 143–5.

nobles whose country houses she visited in the course of her annual progresses. The most famous spectacle of all, the 'Princely Pleasure of Kenilworth' in 1575, was provided by Dudley, who had long had possession of the ancient royal castle of Kenilworth. Although depending at first on the pockets of her nobles, Elizabeth gradually began to spend money more freely herself, especially as she found that the encouragement of piratical enterprise not only evoked a national spirit, but also filled her coffers. While Camden[1] notes a growing tendency to luxury about 1574, others have traced it to the coming of the Duke of Alençon in 1581; certainly the sumptuous entertainments prepared for the welcome of Monsieur were paid for out of the spoils brought back by Drake in the *Golden Hind*. However the Alençon negotiations, whether seriously intended or not, represent Elizabeth's last dalliance with the idea of matrimony. Thereafter she assumed the part of unapproachable virginity which enabled her, as an elderly Cynthia,[2] to maintain a sentimental claim upon the attentions, and the purses, of her youthful servants, without complete loss of dignity. At the same time these later years, which led up to the final triumph over the Armada in 1588, were too strenuous to leave much rooom for revels and for progresses. Elizabeth was an old woman by the time they were over; yet now with the removal of the strain, the spirit of gaiety could break out in full flood.

[1] A contemporary writer and historian.
[2] This is a somewhat pedantic classical allusion, not altogether unexpected in someone who is writing about Renaissance theatre.

DISCUSSION

Rewriting the passage is not nearly as easy as saying what is wrong with it. Not being familiar with the history of the Elizabethan stage you may well have felt this task to be beyond you. Nonetheless the firmer grasp you establish now of the basic principles set out here, the better equipped you will be in the future both to write and read history, and, indeed, to write on other subjects as well.

Returning to the revision of this passage, the secret (as it is with all writing, including your own attempts to write an essay) is this: break the material down into separate single ideas. Though no one can be absolutely sure, through the obscure haze of this passage, just what exactly was in the author's mind, it seems to contain at least twelve separate ideas. In many cases the author, in the original passage, has:

1   Run separate ideas together in one phrase.

2   Failed to distribute the correct emphasis between important ideas and less important ideas.

3   Failed to establish a logical sequence between different ideas showing the manner in which they are related to each other.

These are faults you must yourself try to avoid in any writing which you do.

Apart from his failings in *form*, the author uses obscure words ('liturgies') and references ('elderly Cynthia') and vague, elaborate phrases ('financial stringency') which serve to hide his meaning rather than clarify it. (However it should be said in all fairness that these references were probably very clear to Chambers's original readers.)

The main point, as far as your own writing is concerned, is that you should aim above all at clarity: by all means exploit the infinite richness of the English language: but if you do choose elaborate words and phrases, make sure they are the right ones, that they say exactly what you mean. Do not use such words and phrases merely in an attempt to show off; they are more likely to show you up.

In the revised passage the first sentence is allowed to stand, save for the obscure word 'liturgy'. Liturgy is a technical term from ancient Greece meaning 'a public service undertaken by private citizens at their own expense'. It referred, among other things, to financing the great tragedies and comedies. Chambers means (1) that the spectacles were paid for by private individuals (2) that the Elizabethan Age was comparable to the Great Age of Athens. The next sentence, apart from slight rephrasing of possible obscurities is allowed to stand. There is a main idea: (3) that the most famous spectacle was provided by Dudley at Kenilworth; and a minor one (4) (almost an aside in fact) that the former royal castle at Kenilworth had long been in the hands of Dudley.

The next sentence has been drastically altered. In the original the idea about financial stringency being relaxed (5) seems to be incomplete and isolated. In the revised version it is related back to idea (1) and linked with idea (6) (which comes in rather later in the original) which explains how, through encouraging piracy, Elizabeth was herself able to afford more lavish spectacles. The next idea (7) concerns the two different views as to when the new tendency to lavish expenditure began: in the revised version the use of 'while' introduces the idea of two different views; in the original they are simply set down bluntly without any attempt to fit them in with the rest of the passage. In the revised version we then proceed, without starting a new sentence, to link the luxurious spectacle provided for Alençon with piracy (in this case Drake and the *Golden Hind*) already mentioned (this is (8)). In the original it comes in rather clumsily, the second reference to the Duke (Monsieur) being separated from the first by a rather different general idea (6) about piracy.

The next sentence is practically unchanged save for the addition of the very helpful 'however', which softens the transition from the previous idea, and brings out that having raised the question of luxury we are now turning back to something different, because (9) this is Elizabeth's 'last dalliance'. The idea (10) of Elizabeth's new part, 'unapproachable virginity' is slightly rephrased in order to keep the flow going. For we now move to the idea (also rephrased for the same reason) that we are back again to a period unfavourable to revels and progresses (11). The final idea (12), badly expressed in two separate disjointed sentences in the original, is that although Elizabeth herself is now an old woman, gaiety could again break out: we have already been talking of luxury (and by implication, gaiety) earlier in the reign so the phrase about how 'the spirit of gaiety awoke' (implying that it now appeared *for the first time*) is confusing; the point, apparently, is that it is bigger and better gaiety than before, gaiety 'in full flood'.

This is difficult, gritty stuff, worth puzzling over till you can see clearly why the revised version is better *as communication* (and therefore as history) than the original version.

Perhaps you were yourself successful in writing a revised version. Remember there can be no final, one hundred per cent *correct* version. You *may* have written one which, as *communication* is just as good, which yet differs considerably from the specimen revised version given above. Nonetheless, compare and examine the various versions, and be sure you understand the argument given above for splitting any mass of material down into component ideas, then building a complete passage up from there.

2 SELECTION IN HISTORICAL WRITING

Problems of form and organization are common to any type of writing. Another problem common to all writing, but particularly acute in historical writing, is the problem of *selection*. The past is so rich and complex, and so enormous, that no historian, even if dealing with a relatively short period in time, could set down everything that happened in that time. Nor would he wish to do so. The historian is concerned with those events, and interconnections between events, which are *significant*. The good historian knows which facts to select and which to reject, when he is producing a piece of written history.

It is again impossible to lay down absolute rules. Depending on the kind of history they are writing, different historians will single out different pieces of information as significant.

The passage about the Elizabethan theatre which we studied in the previous exercise might, apart from its formal weakness, have been better had the author employed his powers of selection. For example the phrase about the ancient royal castle having long been alienated to Dudley adds nothing to the main story about the development of the Elizabethan stage and could quite easily have been left out. Similarly the phrase about piratical enterprise affecting the national spirit could also have been left out. And it might have been helpful if the author had *selected* for himself one definite opinion about the date of the 'growing tendency to luxury', instead of shoving down both Camden's version and the version attributing the change to 1581.

Any historian writing a scholarly book will need to consult a vast range of primary and secondary sources but again, of course, he will have to *select* only a small number of passages which are directly relevant to his book. As Dr Kitson Clark has said (you can find out about him in *The Nature of History*, page 144): 'One of the earliest and most painful lessons which a young researcher must master is that much that he has discovered with difficulty, and with some exaltation, will prove in due course to be of no significance and of no imaginable interest, and in the end will have to be left out.'

In writing your own essays as a student you will encounter this very same problem of selection. However hard you have worked, and however much material you have collected, in the end you must be sure to put down in your essay only what is relevant to the subject you are writing about. Often more important than what you put in is what you leave out.

EXERCISE

Imagine you are writing an essay on 'In what ways was western Europe in the sixteenth century becoming more civilized and less cruel?' and you are using as your source (secondary of course) section 5 of chapter 5 of *The Age of Humanism and Reformation* (when you write an essay for real you will, naturally, have to read several chapters in several books). The exercise here is to list the main points from this sub-chapter which do positively show that western Europe was becoming more civilized or less cruel. The idea is to avoid listing points which do not definitely relate to this particular question. Try to arrive at a list of major headings, rather than a detailed list of minor points, names etc., possibly involving overlap and repetition.

SPECIMEN ANSWER

1 Growth and development in some cities, especially Rome, 'so marvellously replanned'.

2 Continuing expansion of communications (lay education and publishing).

3 Cultural, economic and even theological contact across religious divisions.

4 The growth of a sceptical, humane literature.

5 The growth of science.

6 Some hospitals for the sick.

7 Some improvements in the maintenance of order.

8 Humanist questioning of social values, and Catholic and Protestant attempts to establish a socially active Christianity.

9 Flood of popular and bourgeois literature showing that the mental horizons of small traders and artisans were being rapidly enlarged.

10 A rising proportion of Europeans had entered upon a mental world more secular, more varied and more entertaining than that of their forebears and they could live on more than one plane and find new forms of mental escape and solace; there was a quiet enrichment of the daily life of the rapidly expanding mass of literate men and women.

DISCUSSION

Probably in actually writing an essay we would be well advised to start by explaining what we mean by 'more civilized and less cruel' but I hope that the meaning was obvious enough in the context of these few pages by Professor Dickens. I have tried to reduce the points to the smallest number of headings. I think it quite possible that you may have broken things down into more detail. One problem with the headings at the very end is that they rather sum up and indeed include some of the earlier headings: the last point, for example involves, in a sense, a summing up of the effects of expansion of printing, education and economic opportunity, together with the main intellectual and cultural developments. Although the overall growth of wealth probably did contribute to the developments mentioned at the end, on the basis of what Dickens himself writes it would be wrong to include this as a special heading, since he says that this in itself possibly did not prevent a decline in the material standard of living for the majority. Similarly, it would not seem appropriate to select the replacement of mediaeval guilds by private manufacture. Obviously the increasing persecution of witches is an example of how western Europe was becoming *more* cruel, so strictly speaking you should leave it out, or if you felt bound to include it you would have to make this point very clearly.

If you have written down points not included in my headings, check them very carefully to see whether they really are relevant to this topic. (They might well be – as long as you can convincingly defend your own choices, that is fine by me.) This is just intended by way of giving you some practice in selecting what is relevant, and leaving out what is not. Immense amount of detail, for example, on the literary or scientific developments would really show the lack of true powers of selection. This exercise prepares the way for a later one on planning an essay.

3 NARRATIVE, ANALYSIS AND DESCRIPTION

Historical writing can be broken down into three categories: narrative, analysis and description.

Narrative is essential for conveying the sense of change through time which lies at the core of all historical writing (Unit 3, Section 3). Narrative takes us through from an earlier point in time to a later one: in the case of a biography, it takes us from a man's birth, through his childhood, his career, his old age, to his death. In the case of, say, a history of early Florentine humanism a narrative account might start with Petrarch, giving us a chronological account of his life and achievements (1304–74), moving on to Bruni (*c.* 1370–1444) and Alberti (1404–72) adding, respectively, chronological accounts of their lives and achievements, and might perhaps end with a similar treatment for Marsilio Ficino.

A narrative account of industrialization might tell us that Newcomen's steam pump was perfected in 1712; that building of the Carron Ironworks began in 1759; that Hargreaves invented the spinning jenny in 1764, Crompton invented the spinning mule in 1779 and Arkwright waterframe spinning in 1786; that a general upswing in economic activity is clearly detectable from the early 1780s and that Watt invented the rotary steam engine in 1786; that the first census of 1801 suggested that population was increasing rapidly, that some early trade unions were founded in the 1800s, that there was widespread hardship, and that this intensified after the Napoleonic Wars ended in 1815.

This kind of historical writing may have a familiar ring; perhaps you have encountered it in school text books. It is fine, and necessary, as far as it goes, and for some kinds of political and military history narrative may well provide the main drive. The trouble is that although we get the sequence of events, we do not get any kind of description or explanation of them.

When it comes to a history of early humanism a narrative account of names and titles of books simply will not tell us much of the essence and meaning of humanism. Nor is pure narrative form too much help for industrialization. Industrialization cannot be *explained*, cannot be *described*, and its consequences certainly cannot be assessed, by a mere chronological list of inventions and events.

It is the function of *analysis* to deal with these vital questions of explanation, relationship, meaning and achievement. *Description* is in the end perhaps less important than either narrative or analysis, but we do need it sometimes just to tell us what was actually in a particular book or document, or what conditions of life at a certain time were like.

Most often in historical writing, analysis and description will be mingled together. They share a common feature in that while narrative is concerned with change through time, both analysis and description extract some topic from the time process and look at it as if it were static: a narrative account of industrialization lists changes in chronological sequence; description and analysis of industrialization would look at a series of topics in turn – for example 'the cotton industry', 'steam power', 'conditions of the working class', 'factory acts', and so on.

Really we are back to a special problem of *form*. In narrative we divide our ideas, and thus build up our essay, according to time sequence. In analysis and description we divide up our essay according to topic.

Although description and analysis involve the same method of presentation – presentation by topic – and although they are usually mingled together, we can make a clear distinction between them. Analysis performs the more rigorous, intellectual task. Description will tell us what sorts of things Bruni, and Ficino and Machiavelli wrote about; analysis will try to tell us why, by examining the influences on them, and will try to assess the significance of their writings. Description will tell us what working-class conditions in the early nineteenth century were like; analysis will attempt to explain the reasons for working-class misery and squalor and assess whether conditions were better or worse than previously.

In historical writing, if you, or the historian, are to achieve a sense of movement through time, it is always necessary to counterbalance description and analysis on the one side with sufficient narrative on the other side. But in *all* types of writing, including history, if you are to achieve sufficient intellectual rigour, you must counterbalance any narrative and description (the easier aspects) with sufficient analysis.

In many subjects, not primarily concerned with the time factor, narrative can be left out altogether, and it is indeed possible to write history which is almost exclusively analysis and description: the important studies of eighteenth-century politics of Sir Lewis Namier (mentioned in Unit 3, Section 5) are essentially static studies in depth in which the actual period of time covered is so short that there is no need to provide a narrative element. The static quality is well brought out in the very title, *The Structure of Politics on the Accession of George III*. But Namier has been criticized because of this very lack of narrative power, so perhaps we can agree that as *a general rule*, historical writing does require a narrative element.

Summing up we could say:
> pure narrative will almost certainly be bad history;

> pure analysis (as in Namier) *can* be good history, but it is best to aim at a judicious balance between the two (description being included along with analysis).

There are four basic methods of achieving a balance:
1 Divide the material up by topic, but *within each topic observe a narrative sequence*.

2 Alternate passages of narrative with passages of description and analysis.

3 Divide the material up by time sequence into a number of sub-periods, thus giving a broad sense of narrative flow. Then within each sub-period deal with the material topic by topic.

4 'Narrative thickened by analysis' (the phrase is that of Professor G. R. Elton). In general follow a traditional narrative pattern, but whenever a logical need arises for description and analysis, stop the narrative and provide the necessary descriptive and analytical material. This may sound like the best and simplest way, but actually, unless terribly carefully handled, it can lead to an awfully messy piece of writing.

EXERCISE

Let us see if you can work out the practical implications of these approaches yourself. You should by this time have picked up a few general points on the Renaissance, so very roughly and briefly set down in note form what each of these different approaches – listed as points 1–4 in the previous paragraph – would mean if you were writing an essay on the Renaissance (a big topic!). If you don't see what I am getting at here, or if you find the exercise too impossibly time-consuming please just carry on with my answer and discussion – there is no disgrace in that. If you can make a stab at this, my heartiest congratulations.

SPECIMEN ANSWER

1   You would take such topics as:

(a) Turning to Classics – growth of humanism.

(b) Innovations in art and architecture.

(c) Overseas exploration etc.

and within each you would follow a broadly-narrative sequence – e.g. within (c) you would take the different Spanish and Portuguese voyages and conquests in their chronological order, but each time you moved to a new topic you would go back in time and, as it were, start all over again.

2   The sort of scheme suggested here is where you might start off with a narrative account of the rise and development of the Italian city states, particularly Florence, up to the late fifteenth century. Then you could turn to a description of the Italian achievements so far and an analysis of the reasons for them, their significance etc. Then you could continue with a narrative account of the French and other foreign invasions of Italy, stopping in turn for a description and analysis of the achievements of high Renaissance Italy. Broadening the narrative out into other parts of Europe, you might then give an account of events in France, and perhaps give a chronology of the rise of the English nation state. Then once again you could pause for a description and analysis of Renaissance culture in France and England. And so on.

3   You might decide the relevant sub-periods perhaps were: the period of the early Renaissance in Florence (say roughly the early fourteenth century); the period of the spread of the Florentine Renaissance to the rest of Italy (say roughly the late fourteenth century); the period of the spread of the Renaissance to north Europe (say roughly the fifteenth century); the period of the high Renaissance (say the late fifteenth century and the early sixteenth century); the period of the Reformation; and so on. Then within each of these sub-periods you might take in turn economic developments, artistic developments, developments in education, etc., technological developments, overseas developments, etc. In actual practice, you probably would not repeat every topic within every sub-period.

4   Here you would in general follow a traditional political narrative of the changing fortunes of the different European powers. When you were talking of the significance of the Italian city states, you would briefly put in something about Renaissance culture, etc. in these states. When you came to the rise of England, you would briefly put in some analysis and description, say, of the growth of London, and something about, say, the achievements of Shakespeare. And so on.

DISCUSSION

If you did find this exercise practically impossible to do, I hope that now you have seen my specimen answers you understand what is implied in the different approaches one can make to a piece of historical writing.

EXERCISE

A. G. Dickens's *The Age of Humanism and Reformation* has been set partly to give you an example of an extended piece of historical writing at its best. Now see if you can work out the basic plan upon which this book is structured, and the manner in which narrative, analysis and description are integrated together. Obviously in a full length book the plan may be a little more complex than any one of the four alternatives described above.

Very quickly run through the table of contents of *The Age of Humanism and Reformation* and say briefly what approach has been followed in regard to the elements of narrative, analysis and description in each whole chapter and each section of the chapter. Obviously you will not be able to do the whole of this exercise properly if you have not yet managed to read the book, or at least the specially recommended parts of it. But have a bash anyway, just to see if you can get at the underlying structure of a substantial historical work. Again experience has shown that for those of you who are finding Dickens hard going – probably a majority! – this is an impossibly difficult and time-consuming exercise. Once again please do not hesitate to read on. As those of you who meet me at summer school will find out, my way of teaching it is to keep asking questions – even impossible ones! But at least I do give the answers.

SPECIMEN ANSWER

The entire book does have a clear narrative drive, since it starts in the fourteenth century and works its way through to the later sixteenth century, with a post-script on the seventeenth century: roughly, each chapter corresponds to a different sub-period. Chapter 1 is largely analysis, concentrating on one central *topic*, humanism. But a narrative flow is kept up throughout the chapter because each sub-section takes a different sub-period in the development of humanism. Thus we move steadily forward in time from the period before Petrarch to the period of the Florence of the Medicis.

Chapter 1 in effect finishes at the beginning of the sixteenth century. Chapter 2 does not begin exactly at that point, but in fact goes back to the fifteenth century so that there is considerable overlap; however chapter 1 went back into the thirteenth century. Chapter 2 takes us from the beginning of the fifteenth century into the early part of the sixteenth century. But unlike chapter 1, it is not divided into sub-periods following more or less continuously upon each other. Chapter 2 is defined by topic ('States and Nations in Early Modern Europe'), though as a basically political topic this lends itself fairly naturally to a form of narrative treatment. In fact, what happens is that section 1 surveys the entire topic for the whole time span of the chapter, drawing out fundamental comparisons and contrasts: here we have almost pure analysis of the highest order. The remainder of the chapter depends on a special form of division by topic; it is divided up geographically. We then get in turn, 'narrative thickened by analysis and description' first of France, England and Burgundy, then back over the same period for the Iberian Peninsula, and finally back over the same period for Central and Eastern Europe.

The next chapter does not take us very much further ahead in time. Indeed, as one would expect from the title 'High Renaissance Europe' it is in considerable proportion devoted to analysis and description. Basically this chapter, with some considerable overlap backwards in time, takes us up to about 1530. The sub-structure within the chapter is very skilful. Italy had been left out in the previous mainly political chapter, so the first section is a general analysis bringing Italy into relationship with the European countries described in chapter 2. The next two sections come as near to pure narrative of political and military history as anything we get in this richly textured book: in two parts they take us from 1492 to 1513, and then to 1530. However, after this strong underpinning of political and military narrative, we then in section 4 turn to the largely analytic study of 'Art and Letters in Italy', effectively taking matters up where they were set down at the end of chapter 1. In rather similar style the final section then analyses 'Humanism in Northern Europe'. However this analysis of mine does injustice to the way in which Professor Dickens has kept up the narrative drive of the whole book so far by using the development and spread of humanism as a kind of central theme (not a point I would expect you to have noticed in connection with the exercise I actually set; but I hope you do take note of it all the same).

Again in chapter 4 we have the principle of overlap backwards, combined with a general move forward in time. The definition of the chapter is by topic, 'Reformation and Counter Reformation', but it is a topic which suggests development through time. We have arrived at this topic naturally, because it is the consuming issue around 1530, the point in time to which the previous chapter has brought us. The overlap backwards is necessary to properly introduce this particular topic. The sections of the chapter go partly by religious topic, partly by geography, but basically, allowing again for the necessary overlap backwards they represent the progression through a series of sub-periods taking us from the beginnings of the Reformation in the late fifteenth century, right through to the fullest expression of the Catholic Reformation extending into the seventeenth century. The fundamental approach throughout all five sections of the chapter, then, is that of narrative thickened by description and penetrating analysis.

Chapter 5 has its centre of gravity, as it were, further forward in time than chapter 4, and it deals in fuller detail with the late sixteenth century, but again, inevitably, there is some overlap backwards in time. The title 'The Later Sixteenth Century' sounds rather neutral, and might well seem to stress the time element as much as any analysis by topic. But in fact the intention, in part at least, is to provide a kind of basis on which to analyse and sum up the changes which are apparent after the developments described in the previous four chapters. So far (again I wouldn't expect you to have noted this down) the theme driving the book forwards has been the spread and development of humanism, including in chapter 4 its influence on the Reformation. Now, as the very title of the book would suggest, we have the opportunity to assess the combined influence of humanism in its own right, together with the new developments of the Protestant and Catholic Reformations. We start off again with a division into sub-sections on a geographical basis. First, a short, mainly narrative, account of Spain, followed in turn by accounts of England, France and the Netherlands. These mainly narrative sub-sections are then followed by a magnificent piece of analysis 'Social and Intellectual Change in the Sixteenth Century' (which you worked through in a previous exercise).

The book ends with a brief postscript carrying on into the seventeenth century, which is in itself a glowing tribute to Professor Dickens's own belief in dynamic movement and continuity in history.

DISCUSSION

Well, I don't for a moment, expect that you noted things down in quite the way I have done. But I hope you have now gained an insight into the way in which it is necessary to build up a detailed structure for a piece of historical writing, balancing analysis against narrative, and incorporating description where necessary.

The purpose of all this is to help you to understand how history is written by professional historians; it is also intended to help you in forming assessments of your own of the history books which you may encounter on the shelves of a library – how well, you should always ask yourself, has a particular writer organized his material, how well has he balanced and integrated the three main elements of historical writing? Above all, there is this question of organization. You (you will no doubt be relieved to know) will not be called upon to write anything of the scale of *The Age of Humanism and Reformation*, but in whatever you do write the question of organization is extremely important. We saw how in a short paragraph it was necessary to sort out the proper organization of the ideas contained in the paragraph; it is, we have seen, vitally important to organize when writing a book; it is also vitally important to organize when you are writing an essay.

Many students have found this, and the next, section very taxing. If this is so, do not despair. Carry on with the next section, then read the advice I give at the end of it.

4 PLANNING AN HISTORY ESSAY

Perhaps all this business about narrative, analysis and description, and the need to preserve a sense of movement through time, has seemed rather complicated. For the sort of essays you will be called upon to write later on in this course we can offer some rather more simple rules, and ones which will generally serve you well for essays in subjects other than history. (Oswald Hanfling, in Unit 2B, is also giving you advice on these points. For subjects other than history his emphases will sometimes be slightly different, though, of course, we are agreed on basic principles.) Usually, any essay subject which you are set will take the form of asking you a direct question. A first obvious point then is: *always answer the question asked*, not some other question you would like to have been asked, or some other question which relates to the one asked but is not exactly the one asked. To answer the question you will need to analyse your material, not just present straight narrative or description. In writing essays students are often tempted to narrate for nine-tenths of the space at their disposal, then try to make up for this with a solid chunk of analysis at the end. This is a lazy and unsatisfactory way of writing an essay. When you are writing an essay, you should show that you are *thinking all the time*, not simply setting down information. You must, as has already been indicated, be selective in the material you include, making sure it is relevant to the question you have been asked. Finally, you must organize your material, both within individual paragraphs as we have seen, and in the essay as a whole, so that the answer you are giving communicates as effectively as possible with the reader. On the whole (though, of course, not all students are exactly alike in this matter) it is very desirable, in order to achieve a properly organized essay, to set out a plan for it in advance.

Essentially the secret, as with that paragraph about the Elizabethan theatre which we rewrote together, is to try to break the question asked, or your thoughts about it, or (in the case of a history essay) the *relevant* material which you have gathered for the topic, down into meaningful single ideas or headings. Thus, for example, if you are asked the question 'How much did the intellectual and religious ideas of sixteenth-century England owe to continental influences?', you would first of all look around for relevant information in Dickens and among your documents in the Supplementary Texts, but quite probably on the basis of what you already know you could suggest some tentative headings right away. For instance, it might seem sensible to distinguish between intellectual ideas on the one hand, and religious ideas on the other, and to break down intellectual ideas into, say, the separate sub-headings of literature, art and philosophy. After that, an obvious way to structure the essay would be to take first the evidence for continental influence on each of these headings and sub-headings, following this up with a discussion of the evidence showing that these ideas were not influenced by the continent (e.g. the specifically English reasons for the Reformation in England). You might then sum up, perhaps coming to some such sensibly balanced conclusion as that in the main intellectual ideas were influenced by a continental Renaissance save, in part, in the case of Shakespeare where he also drew heavily on the English environment and tradition, but that in the case of religious ideas there is much more of an equal balance between continental influences and native English influences.

But a better way of organizing the essay, which would involve much more comparison and analysis throughout practically every sentence of the essay, would be to take each heading in turn (literature, art, philosophy, religion and any others you have decided on), and with each topic argue out the case for continental influences against English influences.

A plan for an essay along these lines might look something like this:

1   *Literature*
    (a) Continental influences
    (b) English influences
    (c) Conclusions

2   *Art and architecture*
    (a) Continental influences
    (b) English influences
    (c) Conclusions

3   *Philosophy*
    (a) Continental influences
    (b) English influences
    (c) Conclusions

4   *Political ideas*
    (a) Continental influences
    (b) English influences
    (c) Conclusions

5   *Social ideas*
    (a) Continental influences
    (b) English influences
    (c) Conclusions

6   *Religious beliefs*
    (a) Continental influences
    (b) English influences
    (c) Conclusions

7   *Religious organization*
    (a) Continental influences
    (b) English influences
    (c) Conclusions

8   *General conclusions*

That, as you can see, is a very bare and simple plan, and too mechanical to provide a really good essay. However, particularly if you had done some reading on the topic, you might well feel that the sixteenth century was too large to be taken as one single period. You might well want to break it up into sub-periods, such as pre-Reformation, and late Elizabethan (or Shakespearean). The plan of the essay would then be based on a combination of these sub-periods and the topics and arguments already suggested. In making a plan of your own, you would almost certainly want to fill in a little more of the detailed factual information than I have done.

EXERCISE

Now, taking your topics and headings from your reading in Dickens (especially chapter 5 section 5 and the postscript) draw up a plan for an essay on this subject: 'Did western Europe in the sixteenth and seventeenth centuries achieve greater economic prosperity and attain a higher level of intellectual and cultural activity than western Europe in the previous two centuries?' If you skipped the previous two exercises I would like you to attempt this one. But, once more, if you really are reduced to deep misery, then please read on and learn from my answer and discussion.

SPECIMEN ANSWER

Note: This is only one of a very large range of possible plans. It is in no sense definitive. You may well have produced a very different, but equally acceptable plan. I hope you will find it instructive to compare your plan with mine. If you made no headway at all with your own plan, then I hope you can see from my answer how it is possible to go about drawing up a plan. The main purpose of this exercise is to give you practice in designing a plan for an essay, and to show you one example of such a plan.

My plan

1   Introduction

Must distinguish between late sixteenth century and seventeenth century. For purposes of comparison must be clear about characteristics of 'previous two centuries'. Must distinguish between Italy (which, arguably, reached a peak in the early sixteenth century and then went into decline) and the rest of Europe. Must note special cases (e.g. Spain) – Western Europe, in other words, cannot be treated entirely as a unity.

2   Summary of economic and cultural and intellectual characteristics of mid-fourteenth to mid-sixteenth centuries

Economically, fourteenth century a confused period, but some growth of prosperity in fifteenth century. Intellectually and culturally great achievements in Italy, with *Quattrocento* and then high Renaissance at beginning of sixteenth century. Achievements in other countries: Dürer, Erasmus, Sir Thomas More.

3   The late sixteenth century

(a) Some growth in economic prosperity, but enjoyed by minority. Rise of towns, but also decline of some, e.g. Antwerp. Increase in slums. In general life expectations still brief. Advances, then, compared with late fourteenth century, but advance not so significant when compared with fifteenth century.

(b) Printing. This is an invention of the fifteenth century, and its first great expansion took place in the early sixteenth century. Nonetheless there is a continued expansion in the late sixteenth century assisting spread of intellectual ideas. At the same time press is given over to the printing of much rubbish. There is advance here, but clearly building on developments belonging to the earlier period.

(c) Growth of scepticism. Some advance detectable here, yet also continuance of superstition and belief in witch-craft.

(d) Growth of science. Copernicus, Tycho Brahe, Berzelius, Napier. Undoubtedly significant advances here, but note persistence of Aristotelianism, interest in alchemy, and superstitious medical remedies.

(e) Literature. Montaigne, Shakespeare, Rabelais, etc. *Arguably* an advance over anything previously, including Italy, but note, for example, persistence in literature of the Platonic hierarchic universe, together with much mediaeval superstition.

(f) Art and architecture. Over Europe as a whole seems hard to argue that achievements were as great as those of high Renaissance Italy.

(g) Intolerance. There are arguments both ways, but in some ways intolerance increased in the immediate post-Reformation period, compared with the rationality of the high Renaissance period.

4   The seventeenth century

(a) The key argument: this can, with qualifications, be called, in contrast with previous centuries, an age of reason and science. Galileo and Kepler. Bacon, Descartes, Leibnitz and Newton. Yet bigotry and inhumanity continues (Descartes was not against burning witches). Yet some real advance in the spirit of toleration can be seen, particularly towards the end of the century. There are also great advances in political philosophy: Hobbes, Spinoza and Locke. But the question is how do they compare, e.g. with Machiavelli?

(b) The question of economic prosperity. This is the century of the Thirty Years' War involving much disruption and economic distress. This is a period of internal strife in France. It is the period which marks the definitive economic decline of Spain. It is the period of the English Civil War. Yet by the later stages of the century France is clearly emerging into stable relative prosperity under Louis XIV, the Dutch have embarked upon a Golden Age, and in England there is a secure basis for accumulating prosperity. Taken as a whole the century does not stand out as one of notable economic prosperity, but by its end one can see the basis for a greater economic prosperity than ever before.

(c) Art and architecture. Italy, and the rest of Europe, is well launched into the period of the Baroque. Arguably, on balance, this means relatively worse for Italy, and relatively better for the rest of Europe. There are outstanding painters in the rest of Europe: Rembrandt, Claude and Poussin for example.

(d) Literature. With Shakespeare at the turn of the century, then Milton, etc. arguably we only now have the basis for a truly modern literary tradition.

5   Conclusion

On balance the answer is 'yes', particularly with reference to the later seventeenth century, but with many qualifications, particularly in regard to Italy. It has to be stressed, too, how much the achievements of the late sixteenth and seventeenth centuries build on those of the two previous centuries.

Now re-read the note at the beginning of my plan – then ponder this whole exercise very carefully – the writing of a clear, well-organized essay is one of the most important skills expected of the humanities student.

Many students find these last two sections among the most difficult in Units 3–5. If you have not entirely mastered them now, do not worry. Experience shows that they will come to mean more and more to you as you work through the course, when indeed you may wish to come back to them.

5 QUOTATIONS, FOOTNOTES AND BIBLIOGRAPHIES

Whether you are writing an essay, a thesis or a book you must obviously have obtained your information from somewhere. Sometimes you may actually wish to make a direct quotation of a passage which you have found in one of your sources. This is most likely to be so if the passage is from a primary source. For example if you are writing about the Florentine humanists' views of the Renaissance you will very probably need to quote their own words.

Sometimes a passage from a primary or secondary source may seem so striking that you feel you must quote the original. There is another possible reason for quoting directly from a secondary source: it may be that you do not in fact agree with the passage which you are quoting. In this case obviously you must quote the original words so that if necessary you can then go on to disagree with them.

It is important not to overdo the use of direct quotation. 'Scissors-and-paste' is the term we rather contemptuously apply to a piece of historical writing which looks as though the writer has simply cut up chunks of other people's work and pasted them together. Remember that quotations from other authors, however eminent, do not necessarily prove anything. In writing history you must be convinced of the validity of what you are saying. Do not attempt to hide behind quotations from other authors.

Obviously, especially in the early stages of your career, you will be quite dependent on others for most of your ideas: to some extent that is why you are studying in the first place. But you must avoid full-blooded *plagiarism*. This occurs when in fact you steal a phrase from some other writer and pass it off as your own. If you wish to use someone else's phrase then you must use it as a direct quotation – that is either you put it in quotation marks, or you indent it.

The number of times you will wish to use direct quotation will usually depend on the kind of history you are writing. If you are working extensively in primary sources then you may wish to have many direct quotations from these sources. But in your own case – with the sort of essay drawn mainly from secondary sources which you will be writing as a student – there will be less need for direct quotation. In general it is worth memorizing as a basic working rule the statement that *quotations may illustrate a point; they seldom prove it*.

Occasionally the professional historian working in the primary sources does find that a direct quotation from a new document which he has discovered, or from a passage in a document which other historians have ignored or misunderstood, may in fact serve to *prove* the point he is making. More often, for him, as for you, a direct quotation will simply *illustrate* a point rather than prove it. Proof in most cases depends on an argument rather than on one quotation. And this, incidentally, is another reason for stressing form and structure in historical writing. It is the entire presentation of the argument which convinces (or fails to convince) the reader, not isolated facts or quotations.

Apart from merely illustrating a point, direct quotations can often serve a very valuable purpose in conveying atmosphere. You have now encountered a number of extracts from Renaissance documents and, apart from all their other uses, these certainly help to give you the 'feel' of the age in a way in which nothing else can. Direct quotations from letters, diaries, novels, poems, or perhaps folk songs, are often still better for conveying the atmosphere of a particular period in the past.

Here in a brief passage about the Jacobite Rebellion of 1715, taken from *Eighteenth Century England* by Dorothy Marshall, is an excellent example of the use of two brief quotations, one from a song, the other from a diary.

. . . the situation was confused. On 13th November, Argyll and Marr fought an indecisive engagement at Sheriffmuir where, to quote a contemporary song –

> There's some say that we wan; and some say that they wan,
> And some say that nane wan at a', man:

At all events the stalemate continued, so that the Pretender[1] when he finally reached Scotland at the end of the year wrote to Bolingbroke, 'I find things in a prosperous way.' It was wishful thinking based on inadequate knowledge, for by then English preparations had been made for the kill.

[1]The Jacobite claimant to the throne.

An even more impressive example of the use of quotation occurs in Professor G. R. Elton's text book, *England Under the Tudors*, this time to illustrate and drive home a specific point about what he calls the 'Tudor Revolution in Government' (discussed in *The Nature of History* pp. 185–6). You should recognize the document he quotes from!

> The essential ingredient of the Tudor revolution was the concept of national sovereignty. The philosophy underlying Cromwell's work was summarised brilliantly in his preamble to the Act of Appeals (1533), the operative clause of which reads as follows:
>
> 'This realm of England is an Empire, and so hath been accepted in the world, governed by one Supreme Head and King having the dignity and royal estate of the Imperial Crown of the same, unto whom a body politic, compact of all sorts and degrees of people divided in terms and by names of Spirituality and Temporalty, be bounden and owe to bear next to God a natural and humble obedience.'
>
> The critical term is 'empire'. Kings of England had before this claimed to be emperors – the title occurs in Anglo-Saxon times and was taken by Edward I, Richard II, and Henry V – but the meaning here is different. Those earlier 'emperors' had so called themselves because they ruled, or claimed to rule, more than one kingdom, as Edward I claimed Scotland and Henry V France. In the Act of Appeals, on the other hand, England by herself is described as an empire, and it is clear both from the passage cited and from what follows that the word here denoted a political unit, a self-governing state free from (as they put it) 'the authority of any foreign potentates'. We call this sort of thing a sovereign national state.

Now it is this whole question of getting information from sources, whether this information is served up in the form of direct quotation or not, which raises the problem of scholarly apparatus. Quite simply by scholarly apparatus we mean notes, which you will find at the foot of the page in any scholarly work, and bibliographies, which you will find at the end of scholarly books. The purpose of these footnotes and bibliographies should not be to impress you with the dazzling scholarship of the writer of the book. They are intended for use; in identifying the sources from which the author has obtained his information. Wherever there is a direct quotation in a work of scholarship there should be a footnote. More than this: wherever a particular point or idea has been derived from a source, this source should be identified in a footnote. In your own case when writing an essay there will probably be no need for footnotes; but it is important that you should be aware of the principles behind the use of footnotes in scholarly books. Really the point is this: every now and again in reading a book, if you are reading it carefully enough, you should say to yourself 'I wonder how he knows *that*?' The footnote should supply you with the answer.

EXERCISE

1   Professor Dickens uses footnotes in a rather different way in *The Age of Humanism and Reformation*. What is this?

2   Why are there no footnotes of the type I have been describing?

SPECIMEN ANSWER

1   The footnotes explain or elaborate points in the text, or make cross references to other pages in the book.

2   Professor Dickens has written a very wide-sweeping book interpreting large issues rather than a limited work of detailed scholarship. Since almost every statement rests on vast reading, it would be almost impossible to provide succinct footnotes.

In general a bibliography should serve one or other or both, of two functions:

1   As a supplement to, and expansion of, footnote references, presented in systematic and orderly form. In other words a full and clear statement of the sources upon which the historical work concerned is based, designed to satisfy the reader's legitimate desire to know where the author has got his information from, and as a general indication of the reliance which can be placed on the book.

2   As a guide to further reading.

A bibliography of the first type will inevitably be large, and should separate out the various categories of primary sources in accordance with certain principles agreed among scholars which I haven't had time to discuss in these units (but which are described in *The Nature of History*, pp. 133–4 and 155–6. Remember though that since *The Nature of History* is not a set book there is no obligation on you to follow up these references unless you are specially interested). This kind of bibliography is essential to any detailed scholarly work.

A bibliography of the second type is unlikely to include primary sources: though it might include some of the more accessible collections of primary documents, as well as novels, poems, autobiographies, etc. Its main purpose will be to list for the reader the main secondary works which will give him further information on the subject matter of the book. In many cases this sort of bibliography is classified according to topic, or according to chapters of the book. For example the bibliography to the first edition of Henry Pelling's text book *Modern Britain 1885–1955* is divided into the following sections; General, Economic History, Constitutional History, Politics, Social History, Wales, Scotland and Ireland, Foreign Policy, Empire and Commonwealth, War History and Significant Biographies and Fiction.

A good example of the bibliography of the first type is that compiled by E. P. Thompson for his classic study, *The Making of the English Working Class* (discussed in *The Nature of History*, pp. 133–4).

EXERCISE

1   Which type is the bibliography in *The Age of Humanism and Reformation?*

2   How has this bibliography been divided up?

Figure 2   Professor Denys Hay, 1915–

Figure 3   Professor A. G. Dickens, 1910–

SPECIMEN ANSWERS

1   Guide to further reading.

2   By chapter.

The important thing to remember about both footnotes and bibliography is that they are intended for use. As noted on page 123 you will probably not need to include footnotes in your own essays – though on occasion they might provide a convenient way of identifying a particularly striking quotation (remember that you don't want to be accused of plagiarism) or piece of information. If in preparing the essay you have had to read several books, it is quite sensible to list these books at the end as a sort of 'mini-bibliography' enabling whoever is reading your essay to see the sort of authorities you have used in acquiring the information on which the essay is based.

FINAL EXERCISE

This exercise again draws upon the industrialization period. Here is an actual page of historical writing save that the three footnotes have been left out. Indicate with [1], [2] and [3] where you think these essential references should be. Recalling what was said last week about sources, try to guess what sort of sources are referred to in the footnotes.

> Because of its central position in the economy, no sector was more affected than farming by the war which, with two short respites, lasted from February 1793 to July 1815. To the needs of a growing civilian population were added the requirements of a large military force, as well as the help provided to occasionally famine-stricken allies. Apart from the demand for bread or bread-grains, Government contracts in the West Country alone, it is reported, required by 1813 'nearly 400 fat bullocks per week for the Victualling Office, for the Royal Navy, the Prison Ships Garrisons at Plymouth, and the War Prison on Dartmoor' – equivalent to a seventh of the annual sales of cattle at Smithfield. Military requirements also meant extra quantities of leather, tallow, timber, wool, and horse-feed. Horses became expensive early in the war and by 1810 the strangely modern complaint was that they were 'scarce and dear which need not excite wonder, as a foreign slaughter house seems regularly appointed for these animals'.
>
> Part of this enhanced demand was met by increased imports made possible by our command of the seas. Grains from Europe and the U.S.A. supplemented the yields of English fields when crops were poor, and timber from North America partly offset the fall in supplies from the Baltic. The average yearly import of raw wool equalled 3.85m. pounds in 1792–1796 and 7.38m. in 1809–1812, . . .

SPECIMEN ANSWER

> Because of its central position in the economy, no sector was more affected than farming by the war which, with two short respites, lasted from February 1793 to July 1815. To the needs of a growing civilian population were added the requirements of a large military force, as well as the help provided to occasionally famine-stricken allies. Apart from the demand for bread or bread-grains, Government contracts in the West Country alone, it is reported, required by 1813 'nearly 400 fat bullocks per week for the Victualling Office, for the Royal Navy, the Prison Ships and Garrisons at Plymouth, and the War Prison on Dartmoor'[1] – equivalent to a seventh of the annual sales of cattle at Smithfield. Military requirements also meant extra quantities of leather, tallow, timber, wool, and horse-feed. Horses became expensive early in the war and by 1810 the strangely modern complaint was that they were 'scarce and dear, which need not excite wonder, as a foreign slaughter house seems regularly appointed for these animals'.[2]

[1] *The Farmers' Magazine*, XIV (1813), p. 507.
[2] Ibid, XI (1810), p. 128.

Part of this enhanced demand was met by increased imports made possible by our command of the seas. Grains from Europe and the U.S.A. supplemented the yields of English fields when crops were poor, and timber from North America partly offset the fall in supplies from the Baltic. The average yearly import of raw wool equalled 3.85m. pounds in 1792–1796 and 7.38m. pounds in 1809–1812[3], . . .

[3]B. R. Mitchell and P. Deane, *Abstract of British Historical Statistics* (Cambridge, 1962), p. 191.

DISCUSSION

One could, of course, argue that footnotes are required elsewhere as well (in particular after 'annual sales of cattle at Smithfield'), but these three are clearly the essential ones: the first two involve direct quotations, and the third a precise statistical statement.

It would be extremely hard to guess the first two references with any accuracy at all, and you should not worry too much if your answers were completely wrong. Certainly it would be quite possible for these statements to have come from some kind of official government report, though if you guessed that they were from some kind of newspaper or pamphlet or journal (*The Farmers' Magazine* is in fact a journal) you can give yourself a pat on the back.

It should have been easier to guess that the third source was some form of government statistics: in fact the author has gone to a convenient published volume of such statistics, but if you guessed that he had gone to the original Board of Trade returns or something like that, again you deserve a pat on the back.

However if all of these stumped you, don't worry – they are pretty advanced questions. The main point is to understand where, and why, footnote references are necessary in scholarly historical writing.

6 TYPES OF HISTORICAL COMMUNICATION

It is possible to arrange a rough hierarchy of secondary sources (the medium, you will recall, through which the historian communicates his information and interpretation), ranging from the most detailed and scholarly at the top, to those which are so popular and unscholarly that they scarcely merit the title 'secondary source' at all.

Arranged in hierarchical sequence, the types of historical communication which I propose to discuss here are:

1 *The thesis or dissertation*   (Usually written by a postgraduate student for the PhD degree and based almost exclusively on primary sources.) This will be typed, not printed, and will usually be several hundred pages in length.

2 *The learned article*   (Usually the minute examination of one particular topic, published in one of the learned journals – e.g. *The English Historical Review* or *The American Historical Review* – and also based on primary sources.) It will usually be twenty or thirty pages in length.

3 *The scholarly monograph*   (Sometimes this is the same as the PhD thesis, served up as a published book; but generally a published monograph should treat of a subject of greater scope and importance than does the average PhD thesis; it is still mainly based on primary sources.)

4 *The general history*   Self-evidently this is a very broad category. In it I include books ranging from what in *The Nature of History* I have described as 'the interpretative synthesis' to ones which verge on being simply textbooks. The 'general history', in whatever precise form, differs from the monograph in that it deals with a much broader topic. It differs from the text book in that it sets out to make a positive and substantial contribution to knowledge, whereas a text book basically sets out to communicate existing knowledge in as lucid a fashion as possible. The 'general history' both contains primary research and it also *interprets* and *synthesizes* the writings of other historians. In its most impressive form 'the interpretative synthesis' presents some striking new general idea covering a quite broad area of historical study – as for example R. R. Palmer's idea of the Atlantic-wide 'Democratic Revolution' in his *The Age of the Democratic Revolution* (discussed in *The Nature of History*, p. 160). A. G. Dicken's *The Age of Humanism and Reformation* does not quite fulfil exactly that function, yet it is clearly much more than just a text book, particularly in the way in which it stresses the development of humanism, and the linked development of the Reformation as underlying general ideas. A book we quoted earlier (p. 123), G. R. Elton's *England Under the Tudors*, was designed as a text book, but because of the weight of original research and, above all, the special 'Eltonian' interpretation which governs the book, this too is really a general history.

5 *The text book*   (Naturally text books can be written for a variety of different age-groups and audiences. But leaving aside the more elementary books which, in any case, involve problems of educational psychology as much as history, we can regard text books covering fifth form to university teaching as roughly in the same category.) Though all history, including text books, must in the last analysis be the historian's own interpetation, and can never be a completely objective statement of accepted knowledge, the basic task of the text book is to provide clear, simple coverage of some period or topic, in accordance with the best existing knowledge. It will draw largely on secondary sources though the author may very probably be a primary expert in the period.

Additionally there is a type of text book devoted to the provision of extracts selected from primary sources (the source book), or excerpts from a range of secondary sources (the collection of readings). Though you might note that Lawrence Stone's *Social Change and Revolution in England 1540–1640*, discussed in *The Nature of History*, p. 212, is an example of the latter, we need not bother with this type of book meantime. Your Course Reader, *Nature and Industrialization* is, in essence, a source book as are the Supplementary Texts.

6   *Pop history*   History written for a wider audience is perfectly respectable provided it is written honestly, and provided it is accepted for what it is. Nowadays professional academic historians, as well as journalists, participate in the writing of pop history, whose most recent form is best seen in the illustrated history magazines, such as Purnell's *History of the First World War*. Radio and television have provided the opportunity for a still more up-to-date form of pop history.

Film, radio and television, seriously presented, can also provide a form of historical communication which comes nearer to a text book, or even to a work of general history, than it does to pop history – where the basic rationale, of course, is that it should have value as *entertainment*.

7   *The historical novel*   Strictly speaking this is not acceptable as a type of history – by definition, after all, it is fiction – and you should not think of the historical novel as, in any real sense, history. But there is so much confusion surrounding the question of the historical novel that it is worth glancing at it here.

Remember of course that a novel, whether an historical novel or not, can be a valuable primary source, but that is a different question from its role as a piece of historical communication. What one can say about the historical novel in terms of communication is that at a rather elementary level it may serve a useful purpose in arousing interest in a particular historical topic or in conveying atmosphere and background information about a particular period. It is in this sense that the novel *Gone with the Wind* has (believe it or not) been praised as having value in the teaching of history because the descriptions of the American Civil War are not only colourful but fairly reliable. But no one can really compare such passages in a novel with a serious historical study of the Civil War.

Mention of *Gone with the Wind* reminds me that the historical feature film is in many ways akin to the historical novel in that it may also arouse interest and convey a certain amount of atmosphere. The British film of the 1960s *The Charge of the Light Brigade* might possibly be regarded in this sense. But from the historian's point of view the real interest of *The Charge of the Light Brigade* is not what it tells us about the Crimean war (there are many far more reliable sources for the Crimean war) but for what it will tell the future historian about the attitudes of British film makers in the 1960s (above all an anti-heroic attitude, and a kind of detailed 'realism' – though when it came to such matters as uniforms there were many inaccuracies).

Really what is at issue in this attempt to classify different types of historical communication is the aims that the particular writer has in mind. There is no point in blaming a man for having written a colourful but unreliable piece of history if in fact all he has set out to do is to entertain or perhaps to make some money for himself. In assessing any piece of historical writing what one must do first of all is decide what kind of history the writer is trying to produce, then judge the particular work on that basis. One is certainly entitled to be very critical of a book which has really been written purely to entertain or to make money for the author but which tries to claim that it is a genuine contribution to historical knowledge.

A valuable distinction can be made between writing history and mere bookmaking: bookmaking arises when someone feels that it would be nice to write a book without really having any very strong wish to further knowledge or to communicate particular information; the book in fact might be about anything, it

Figure 4   Trevor Howard as General Lord Cardigan in the film, Charge of the Light Brigade, *apparently wearing the uniform of a cornet (see Figure 5) (Photograph supplied by National Film Archive; reproduced by courtesy of United Artists Corporation Ltd).*

Figure 5   Cornet Wilkins of the 11th Hussars, 1855 (National Army Museum).

just so happens that it is about an historical topic. Such books, despite the intentions, may in fact turn out to be valuable as historical communication at a fairly low level, but they may on the other hand deserve our severest criticism. In general, professional historians, rightly, tend to distrust the work of a man who one year writes a book about the twentieth-century novel, and the next year, say, a book about Magna Carta.

The main purpose of this classification is to enable you to distinguish between different types of history and to criticize them intelligently. You should thus be able to get the best out of whatever kind of history you are reading or, in the case of a film or television programme, watching.

EXERCISE

Distinguish between the different types of history contained in the following list by entering the appropriate number, 1–6 as defined above in the box provided. Write down a brief comment explaining your choice.

Note that the novel has been excluded as *not* being a genuine type of historical writing.

A   A twenty-four page piece of historical writing, containing a total of sixty-one footnote references, entitled, 'The recognition of Pope Alexander III: some neglected evidence.'

B   G. R. Elton, *England Under the Tudors*.

C   A book from which the following is the opening passage:

'There were boats on Loch Leven when John Forbes reached the narrows at Ballachulish. They lay like curled leaves on the dark water, high at the stem and stern, and almost motionless as the oarsmen pulled against the drag of the tide and the tug of the wind. They were ferrying soldiers across from Carness, and when Forbes saw the slant of pikes and the burnished barrels of muskets his memory stirred uneasily. At first there was nothing by which he could identify the soldiers, only the scarlet of their coats in the winter's grey light. Riding closer to the ferry he saw the goat's-head badge on their bonnets, the green plaids in which some of them were wrapped, and he recognised them as men of the Earl of Argyll's Regiment of Foot. When the first files waded through the shallows and formed up with their faces towards Glencoe he felt more uneasy still.'

D   A four-hundred-page book entitled *The Crisis of the Early Italian Renaissance*, of which the following is the opening passage:

'The method of interpreting great turning-points in the history of thought against their social or political background has not yet rendered its full service in the study of the Italian Renaissance. To be sure, the long accepted view that the emergence of Renaissance culture stood in close relationship to the rise of a new civic, or bourgeois, society has

130

proved fruitful in many fields of Renaissance research; and equally useful has been the knowledge that the late Renaissance was molded[1] by a new courtly society, first in the Italy of the signories and principates, and later in the great European monarchies of the six-teenth century. But neither viewpoint helps to explain the fact that one of the greatest forward-strides occurred about the year 1400.'

E   A book, entitled *The USA Since The First World War*, which is part of a series of 'Twentieth-Century Histories'. The work is described by its publishers in the following manner:

'Steeped in his subject, Mr. Hill is able to con-centrate on the essentials, illustrating with per-tinent detail where needed, yet never obscur-ing the broad outline of the story. This is designed not only to reveal how the United States came to leadership of the Western World, but also to give some understanding of how the American citizen feels about it and about his own domestic problems, such as social security or Negro rights.

'Mr Hill surveys the economic collapse of 1929 and the Great Depression, Roosevelt's dynam-ism contrasted with Hoover's inability to mobil-ise the resources of government, the exper-iment of prohibition and the gangsterism to which it gave rise. Recovery and the massive development of American industry as the arsenal of democracy, the American story of the Second World War, McCarthyism and the Cold War, Kennedy, Khrushchev and Cuba. It is all there in a tense and vigorous narrative. For bet-ter understanding Mr. Hill has provided an appendix on the working of the American sys-tem of Government.'

F   A three-hundred-page book, *The Road to 1945: British Politics and the Second World War*, by Paul Addison.

G   A book from which the following paragraph is quoted:

'It was not until the second half of the eighteenth century that the change towards large-scale industry quickened, becoming so rapid as to appear revolutionary. A number of interconnected causes produced this accel-eration. There was a growth of population, creating an increased demand for goods. There was improved transport, making possible the carrying of finished commodities to markets and raw materials to centres of production. There were the great mechanical inventions, new materials, and improved chemical processes, which quickened and cheapened production. It is useless to try to assign priority to any of these

[1]This is an American book with American spelling.

131

factors; together they comprised the Industrial Revolution.'

H   A four-hundred-page typed, but not printed, work entitled, 'Political Change in Britain September 1939 to December 1940'.

ANSWERS AND DISCUSSION

Passage A   2

This is in fact the title of an article in the July 1969 issue of *The English Historical Review*. Note that it is only twenty-four pages long: obviously an article, not a book or a thesis.

Passage B   4 or 5

We had a quotation from this book on page 123, where it was identified as a text book, and it was referred to again on page 127, where I said it was really a general history. So you see I have difficulty in making up my own mind too, sometimes. What I really want you to get from this exercise is the broad distinction between detailed very scholarly history and more general and popular works.

Passage C   6

This is a work of popular history (John Prebble's *Glencoe*). It is over-romanticized. It is extremely unlikely that some of the things the author says could have been drawn from reliable source material – e.g. 'his memory stirred uneasily'. Remember the question you must always keep asking when you read a work of history: 'How does he know that?'

Passage D   4

The title, together with the introductory lines quoted, should make it clear that the author is aiming at a great new work of interpretative synthesis, highly original, but broader than a mere monograph. However, I certainly couldn't blame you if you said 3.

Passage E   5 or 6

To *me* it is clear from the material quoted that this is one of a series of fairly elementary text books, but I agree that it could equally well be 6, pop history.

Passage F   3

This is the recent standard monograph on British politics in the Second World War, of such breadth, however, that it might almost be considered a general history, save that the time-scale is rather too specific and restricted. But I would also give you full marks for 4.

Passage G   5

This is more difficult, but the rather simplified, matter-of-fact style should clearly reveal it as a text book. Facts are presented, but the last sentence rather explicitly disavows any real attempt at explanation. I couldn't really blame you if you put 3, 4 or 6.

Passage H   1

This, as you might guess, is the thesis which Paul Addison wrote before proceeding to the further research and reading necessary for the production of his standard monograph, *The Road to 1945*. It is typed, not published.

7 PERIODIZATION AND HISTORICAL SEMANTICS

In planning a piece of historical writing it is often useful, as we have seen, to divide the entire material up into a number of sub-periods. We have already discussed comparisons between 'The Seventeenth Century' and 'The Sixteenth Century', and we have had references to 'The Renaissance period', and to 'The Middle Ages'. One of the fundamental things the historian is always doing is dividing up the past into periods, whether large or small. In fact this process of periodization is absolutely essential to the historian's activities. The past is so complex and contains such an enormous mass of material that it would not be possible for the historian to deal with it at all if he did not, as it were, chop it up into convenient chunks, or periods.

Of course this convenient habit of the historians has many dangers. The past is really continuous: you do not fall asleep in a period called 'the middle ages' and wake up the following day to find that you are in 'the modern world'. The historian must beware of extreme pronouncements about a new age or a new era suddenly beginning. This in fact is one of the problems you have probably already encountered in the more elementary kind of historical text book where the author's attempt to be clear and simple has led to an undue stress on the breaks between one historical period and another.

The point to be made is that periodization is useful and indeed essential, but it has many dangers and so must be approached with considerable care.

The most rough and elementary, yet basic, form of periodization may possibly be well-known to you: that into ancient, mediaeval and modern. This most useful classification roughly divides the history of Western civilization into:

1   the period prior to the final collapse of the Roman Empire in the west – the ancient world;

2   the period between this collapse and the beginnings of certain changes which you have already got used to describing as the Renaissance – the middle ages;

3   the period since the Renaissance – the modern world (some historians, of course, say that the Renaissance is in itself a period of comparable significance).

It is important to note right away that this classification is only valid for Western civilization. It takes no account whatsoever of developments in Nigeria, say, or China, or South America; that is to say, it ignores vast and important areas of human experience. The other problem in regard to this classification arises when we try to place precise boundaries or definitions on these various terms, ancient, mediaeval and modern. Remember again that no piece of historical writing should ever suggest that on one day one period came to an end, and that on the next a new one began.

The 'ancient, mediaeval, modern' classification was invented by those Italian intellectuals you have already encountered in chapter 1 of *The Age of Humanism and Reformation*. These intellectuals, as we saw from that letter written by Marsilio Ficino, were conscious of a 'golden age' in which classical learning had been revived, or of a rebirth, or 'Renaissance' as Vasari (check up on him in Dickens) called it. These intellectuals tended to write off the centuries after the fall of Ancient Rome as 'the middle ages'.

It is all right for us to talk of 'the middle ages' as long as we do not imply that in some way life in the middle ages was inferior to that of the ancient world or of the modern world. Although ultimately, as we have seen (Unit 3, section 6), the historian is bound to make some sort of judgements of this kind, he first has a duty to understand a past age on *its own terms:* he should not look upon the mediaeval world (that is, the middle ages) as some kind of museum of curiosities.

133

Too often, too, universities and schools have treated ancient history as belonging to the world of the classics, rather than to history, again emphasizing the idea of a sharp break. One of the most rewarding developments today in the study of history is the way in which ancient history is treated as a part of history in general, bringing out the continuities, rather than the sharp breaks, in human experience.

EXERCISE

Listed below are various passages related to the question of periodization which you might find in various kinds of historical writing. Indicate which ones you feel conform to the highest standards of historical writing (A), which ones you feel, given fuller explanation and qualification, are probably acceptable (B), and which ones you feel to be quite unacceptable (C). Write a short comment on each.

1　'September 1931 marked the watershed of English history between the wars. Though any division of time above a year is arbitrary, arising only from our habit of counting with arabic numerals by ten, decades take on a character of their own. What was at first merely a convenience for historians is accepted as a reality by ordinary men when they become more literate and judge the world more from books and newspapers than from their own experience. The "twenties" and the "thirties" were felt to be distinct periods even at the time, and September 1931 drew the line between them. The break can be defined in many ways. The end of the gold standard was the most obvious and the most immediate. Until 21 September 1931 men were hoping somehow to restore the self-operating economy which had existed, or was supposed to have existed, before 1914. After that day, they had to face conscious direction at any rate so far as money was concerned.'

2　'In 1914 an old world perished. In 1918 a new one came into being.'

3　'So far only a few exceptional men were conscious of this transition, but as time went on awareness of it spread, partly for reasons which we shall notice later, until it came to be generally believed that there had been great changes in or soon after the late fifteenth century in all the mutable parts of human nature. A great historian completed the idea by inventing the name "the Renaissance", the rebirth, under which he tried to group together, as aspects of the revival of antiquity, all the revolutionary changes of those days, not only those which we have mentioned, but also others to which we have still to come. This idea, like the idea of the Middle Ages, did good service, if only in reminding historians how every department of human life is influenced by every other; but it also did harm by leading to fanciful comparisons between the naive, superstitious men of the ages of faith, whose universe seemed to them familiar and friendly, or at least accessible to conciliation by means of the Church; and the men of the Renaissance, fearless and free, asserting the rights of the individual, pouring out a defiant literature of which Man was the hero, or substituting the cold certainties of science for the comforts of religion. Such interpretations of history try to compress into a phrase and discern in a short stretch of years changes which are never alike in any two men, which are never complete in any one man, which draw their sinuous course through many generations. Continuities are never wholly broken. Many medieval habits and beliefs and institutions persisted until much later; some of them survive, but little altered, in our own time. The Renaissance was gathering force in the twelfth century, and it is still being continued by archaeologists, by grammarians, by artists, and by thinkers.'

4　'In October 1760 George III came to the throne; the age of industrialization had begun. Peaceful agricultural life gave place to the bustle of great towns and cities.'

5　'With the Battle of Bosworth the modern history of England began. Henry VII's predecessors were mediaeval in policy and outlook; he was the first king to follow modern policies.'

SPECIMEN ANSWERS

Passage 1   A
This is a very sophisticated piece of historical writing, taken from A. J. P. Taylor's *English History 1914–1945* which actually goes to some lengths to explore, as it were, the philosophy underlying the idea that the twenties and the thirties are distinct periods of time.

Passage 2   B
As it stands this is a very blunt statement, which without further explanation and qualification we would be inclined to distrust, so I would also give you full marks if you said C.

Clearly it contains just about as much exaggeration as is permissible in this sort of remark: pinning the perishing of the old world to one year (1914), and the coming into being of the new one also to one year (1918) is rather extreme. On the other hand what presumably lies behind the statement is the suggestion that it was really the four years of war (1914–18) which brought about this sharp change; and this is quite a reasonable suggestion to make, if we remember that in strict reality an old world can no more perish completely than an entirely new one can come into being.

Passage 3   A
Again this is an extremely subtle piece of historical writing, taken from G. N. Clark's *Early Modern Europe*. What this boils down to is a quite excellent statement of the problems involved in trying to pin down exactly when 'the Renaissance' took place, one of the sixty-four-million-dollar questions as far as periodization is concerned.

Passage 4   C
This statement is just plain daft. Industrialization – the change from agricultural to town life – could not possibly have taken place as suddenly as this, and in any case could have little to do with the accession to the throne of a particular king.

Passage 5   C
This one is almost as daft. The switch from mediaeval to modern could not possibly take place as suddenly as is suggested here. Even if we could agree what we mean by 'mediaeval' and what we mean by 'modern' it is obvious that Henry VII's predecessors must have been 'mediaeval' in some things, 'modern' in others; and similarly with Henry VII himself. The statement is not as bad as passage 4 because it is at least arguable that (once we have agreed on definitions for 'mediaeval' and 'modern') in the end Henry was more 'modern' than 'mediaeval' while his predecessors were more 'mediaeval' than 'modern': I would not regard you as wrong, therefore, if you stuck out for B.

DISCUSSION

For reasons just given, you need not worry too much if you have given passage 5 a B, though you should read the critical comment given above very carefully. And as I have noted you might have felt inclined to give passage 2 a C. Again that would be reasonable, though for reasons given I think that it just scrapes through (one takes it that the author would in fact provide the necessary elaboration and qualification). Passage 4 can be nothing but C; and passage 3, of course, nothing but A. You may have had some reservations about passage 1 feeling that, despite his careful explanation, Mr Taylor still overstresses 'the watershed': if so you would be entitled (though I think you would be wrong) to put passage 1 in the B class. Remember what has been said already about the difficulty of making one hundred per cent decisions about historical writing.

Because of the difficulties in handling the word 'Renaissance', some historians have preferred to try to avoid it. The book we used to use, covering the period of the Renaissance and Reformation, was simply entitled *Early Modern Europe*. Professor Dickens refers to the problem on his opening page. In fact the Renaissance is as much a label as a period. And this takes us into the realm of historical semantics.

'Semantics' means 'the study of the meaning of words'. There is no need whatsoever for you to embark on such a study. But it is very important that you should appreciate the difficulties which arise in historical writing from the use of such 'labelling words' as 'Renaissance', 'humanism', 'reformation', 'revolution', 'romanticism', 'feudalism', 'capitalism', 'radical'. Every time we use one of these words we are involved in a semantic problem, that is to say, a problem involving the meaning of the particular word used.

Such words are essential in historical writing: pick up any history book and you will find dozens of them. But often they are used in such a vague, imprecise way, that instead of contributing to the communication of historical understanding they merely contribute to confusion.

There are six main points to notice in historical semantics:
1   Words which did actually exist in the periods of the past about which the historian wishes to write, but which, down through the ages, have changed in meaning. Example: 'radical'.
2   Words which have been invented later to describe something in a past age, but *which were actually unknown to the people of the time*. Example: 'feudalism'.
3   Words which we use loosely in everyday speech, which, because of their vagueness, can be confusing when used in a historical context. Example: 'the people'.
4   Words used to suggest a form of periodization. Example: 'the Renaissance'.
5   Words which exist in one language, but do not have an exact equivalent in another language. The translation, therefore, will be inexact and likely to give rise to confusion. Example: the Russian word *Krepostnoi*, usually translated as serf, though in fact the Russian serf was completely different from the mediaeval English serf.
6   'Geographical abstractions'. Example: 'Europe' – historians do talk about, say, 'Europe in the tenth century', though in fact people at the time were scarcely aware of a geographical area called Europe; they tended instead to talk about 'Christendom'.

One of the most troublesome of the words which have changed in meaning (point 1), and one which you will encounter in the final third of this Foundation Course, is 'radical'. In strict accordance with the derivation of the word from the original Latin, a radical is someone who advocates reform 'by the roots', that is to say extreme reform. In Britain in the early nineteenth century the word was used of those who opposed the existing political system, and in fact covered a pretty wide range of opinions. However, the word became particularly associated with politically active middle-class figures who desired among other things: (a) as much reform in the political system as would give them the vote; (b) removal of traditional restrictions on industry and trade; and (c) reform of the antiquated legal system. In the later nineteenth century radical usually meant the more extreme members of the Liberal Party, though earlier there had been 'Tory radicals' who showed a greater interest in social questions (e.g. factory reform) than did the Conservative or Tory Party in general. Radical issues, however, remained largely middle-class issues; by the early twentieth century radicalism was beginning to seem old-fashioned compared with the growth of Labour politics and socialism. Today 'radical' usually means someone who holds views of a more extreme character than those of the majority of his own political party; but to give the word any kind of precise meaning it is necessary to add a further qualifying word: e.g. 'Liberal radical', 'radical socialist', 'Christian radical', 'Radical Socialist' – a specific political label in the French parliamentary context.

In France the term 'radical' actually became the official title of a political party, which, in the main, stood in alliance with the independent French peasantry for moderate middle-class reformism. The association with middle-class interests, then, both in France and Britain and elsewhere is a strong one. But it is important to remember that 'radical' is a political label describing (often somewhat vaguely) a man's political opinions, *not his social class*. An aristocrat, or a worker, could be a radical (though note, equally, that radicalism does *not* generally connote a working-class movement); if you want to pin a man down by his social class, or economic position, call him 'middle-class', or 'a professional man', or 'a banker', or whatever he is.

The best example of the second type of problem is the word 'feudalism' (along with the adjective 'feudal' and the phrase 'feudal system'). This word was first used in the eighteenth century to describe the somewhat ill-defined social structure which existed in Europe for several centuries from about the tenth century onwards. There was never a complete 'system' in the sense of a rigid pattern of social relationships conforming to certain definite 'rules'; and, of course, the label used by later historians was quite unknown to men actually living at the time.

Yet without any doubt a social structure did exist in these centuries clearly and identifiably different from the social structures of earlier or later periods. It is possible to pin down some of the essentials of feudalism with some such form of words as 'it was a system of social relationships in which inferiors held land of their superiors by virtue of performing some service for their superior; to begin with, for example, knights held land from their lords in return for performing military service'. Thus the word 'feudalism' serves a very useful purpose as a 'label' describing something which is in fact quite complicated. But since the word was not known to the men who actually lived in the period of what we call 'feudalism', clearly there are times when we must handle the word very carefully. For example if we wish to say (and we might, provided we supplied plenty of explanation and qualification): 'The barons objected to Edward I's anti-feudal policies' we would have to remember that to neither Edward I nor to the barons could the word 'anti-feudal' have any meaning, and that, therefore, it might be better to spell out in more detail the exact nature of the policies to which the barons objected.

Whenever you are writing a history or taking part in a serious discussion of historical matters switch on the mental red light if you find yourself talking about 'the people' (point 3). Ask yourself what exactly you mean. Every single person in a particular country? A majority of them? All of them except the king? All of them except the rich? The working class? Quite probably you are not really sure what you do mean, which, naturally, means that what you are writing or saying is not very good history.

Whether or not you do know what you mean, a pause for thought is called for. Almost certainly instead of the vague 'the people' you could substitute something more precise such as 'a majority of the people', 'the middle and working classes' and so on.

Another word which lends itself to the same sort of loose usage is 'the masses'.

And of course there is even a good deal of vagueness about phrases like 'the middle classes', 'the working classes', which in fact involve a mixture of problems (1), (2) and (3), but which are probably best discussed here, since we do in fact make extensive use of them in everyday language.

The phrases 'middle class' and 'working class' (or better, 'middle classes' and 'working classes') came into general use in the early nineteenth century when the 'Industrial Revolution' had created a 'middle class' of people whose wealth was drawn from industry and commerce instead of (as was the case with the aristocracy or 'upper class') from land, and a 'working class' whose sole source of income was from their labour in the industrial factories. In earlier periods people talked, not of classes, but of 'estates' or 'orders' or of someone's 'station in life'. There is no harm in using the phrase 'middle class' for these earlier periods to describe what contemporaries might perhaps refer to as 'the middling sort of people' – merchants, tradesmen, lawyers, such business men as existed – provided it is realized that the phrase was not used by people at the time, and that in different periods the phrase will apply to different sorts of people. One of the most banal lapses into which students (and teachers!) of history too often fall is to talk of 'the middle class' as if it remained the same throughout the centuries. For pre-industrial periods the phrase 'the working class' will probably not be terribly helpful: better to say, 'the peasants', or 'the labourers', or 'the poor', depending on which you mean.

The problem of historical semantics joins up with the problem of periodization (point 4) the moment a label is given to a particular period, as in 'The Renaissance' or 'The Enlightenment' (for the eighteenth century). One important question to ask right away is: was the label invented by men at the time, or was it a later invention of historians? Both 'The Renaissance' and 'The Enlightenment' have widespread acceptability because they are phrases which contemporaries actually used. In his *Lives of the Artists* (check in Dickens), Vasari, writing in the middle of the sixteenth century, actually used the word *renascita* – rebirth or renaissance. However for him the stress was on the *re*, the rediscovery of the best features of the ancient world, a return to something *old*. A modern historian, on the other hand, still using the word 'Renaissance' tends, as we have seen, to lay stress on the *new* approaches developing in this period, leading to the modern world of science, of individualism, and of independent nation states.

Problems arising from translation, and 'geographical abstractions' are less important for the moment (points 5 and 6). If you are bothered, you can read about them in *The Nature of History*, pp. 167–8.

When you yourself write a history essay you will find that you have to make use of the phrases discussed above, or others like them. Each time you must be absolutely clear in your own mind what concrete meaning lies behind the phrases you use. There is no point talking about 'the Radicals' or about 'Capitalism' unless you know what, in terms of real historical people, real events and real processes, these phrases signify. Too often, of course, students (and others!) use phrases like these because they think they sound good, without really being clear about their meaning. Remember: if you don't know what you mean, whoever is reading your work won't know what you mean either.

Always consider: what would you say if asked what it means.

EXERCISE

Apart from the word 'Renaissance' itself, two labelling words run throughout Professor Dickens's book, together with a further one closely linked to the second of these words. Professor Dickens gave precise attention to the definition of two (but not all three) of these 'historical labels'.

1 What are these 'historical labels'?

2 Why are only two defined?

3 What are the definitions given by Professor Dickens?

Figure 6   R. M. Hartwell, 1921–

Figure 7   Professor E. J. E. Hobsbawm, 1917–

SPECIMEN ANSWERS

1   'Humanism', 'Reformation', and 'Counter Reformation'.

2   'Humanism' and 'Counter Reformation' are the ones which obviously give rise to difficulties and ambiguities. As Professor Dickens puts it (page 182) 'the term Counter Reformation . . . might well be regarded as a simplification even more drastic than most such historical labels'. The term Reformation, on the other hand, can be seen as a rather more straightforward and obvious one, whose meaning arises naturally from the first sections of chapter 4.

3   Humanism is defined briefly on page 4 as 'A creative study of Greek and Roman civilisation'. The word is developed and redefined throughout the book as a part of Professor Dickens's basic thesis that humanism itself constantly developed and was alive to new problems; it was not a merely pedantic study of the classics. (It might be noted, incidentally, that as with feudalism the word 'humanism' was unknown to the people of the period – i.e. the fourteenth, fifteenth and sixteenth centuries. The contemporary origins of the concept lie in the word 'humanist' (*umanista*), meaning, as Professor Dickens also tells us on page 4, a teacher of the *studia humanitatis*.)

The term Counter Reformation, and the whole basic problem of whether we should not more accurately speak of the Catholic Reformation, is discussed on page 182.

EXERCISE

Jot down any other historical labels which occur to you, and attempt to say what you mean by them (or discuss the problems involved in trying to define them).

SPECIMEN ANSWERS

Here are just a few of the more obvious ones you have already discovered, or will be likely to discover:

Empire

This word has generally come to connote an area of territory in which one country or nation exercises power over other countries or nations, though in the Tudor period as you may recall from a paragraph from Professor Elton's *England Under the Tudors* the word was simply used to apply to the English nation state. What this means is that the student of Tudor England must exercise caution when he comes across this word in a primary document. Otherwise the modern meaning is fairly clear. Sometimes, however, we get the additional emotional complication, often inseparable from this type of problem, that empire is now often regarded as being rather a bad thing and therefore may be used almost as a term of abuse.

Romanticism

You will encounter this term in the postscript to *The Age of Humanism and Reformation*. Most historians are agreed that towards the end of the eighteenth century a general movement in ideas and the arts began which had certain definite and common characteristics which can reasonably be described as 'romantic'. Included in these characteristics are: (1) a general turning away from formal classical ideals towards a greater emotionalism and freedom of expression; and (2) a turning away from the harsh reality of the contemporary world towards the beauties of nature, or towards an alleged Golden Age in the past, or towards a hoped-for Golden Age in the future.

Capitalism

This word has specially marked emotional overtones because of its usage by Marxist historians. It can however be used in a fairly neutral way simply to describe a type of economic organization in which the most important persons are the owners of the capital upon which commerce and industry is based (as distinct from the owners of land). See Dickens, p. 44.

Laissez-faire

This French phrase was first used in the eighteenth century to describe a policy of freedom from the economic restrictions which had been a characteristic of the mediaeval and early modern period. It came into general usage in Britain in the nineteenth century to characterize a particular type of social and economic policy which insisted that it was best for the government not to interfere in social and economic matters but to leave such matters to the free operation of private enterprise.

Bourgeois

Again this word tends to figure in Marxist historical writing. Originally meaning 'townsman' it is used most often simply as a synonym for middle class.

Industrialization

The process by which a country's economy becomes dependent on industry rather than agriculture; thus the phrase also implies the change from country life . to town life based on the development of industry.

Industrial Revolution

It is usually accepted that this phrase was brought into general usage by Arnold Toynbee (uncle of the more famous A. J. Toynbee who died in 1975) lecturing in the 1880s. Although for a time in the 1930s historians tried to do without the phrase (just as historians for a time tried to do without the phrase 'The Renaissance' – see Dickens, p. 3) it is now equally accepted that it usefully describes an important series of events and relations between events taking place sometime in the late eighteenth century and early nineteenth century. In a real sense these events had revolutionary implications in that there was a definite and identifiable change in the way of life of the majority of the British people.

Socialism

Again socialism can have marked emotional overtones. It was often used in the nineteenth century simply to mean state action in economic and social matters. But in its best usage it implies such action positively on behalf of the working classes. Thus it implies some kind of philosophy aiming at a reconstruction of society. However, it remains a difficult word in that all sorts of different people who say they believe in socialism turn out to mean all sorts of different things by this phrase. The rule is, as with all of these semantic problems, be sure yourself what you mean, and be sure that your reader knows what you mean. Socialist is no more a synonym for 'working class' than 'radical' is for 'middle class'.

Always be aware that, in history, you cannot just shuffle labels around as you might shuffle a pack of cards. It is very easy in historical writing to produce vague phrases which lack any clear and definite meaning. Really the fundamental point of this discussion is to drive home the point that in writing history and in writing anything else (though obviously in literature and art history there is more scope for impressions and intuitions, where personal reactions and values may be more important than hard facts or analysis) you must always be as clear and definite as you can. Avoid 'waffle'. Aim to be *concrete* and *precise*.

8 CONTROVERSY IN HISTORICAL WRITING

There are many famous controversies in history. 'Why did the American colonists rebel against the British Government?' 'What exactly was the Renaissance and when did it take place?' 'Did the Industrial Revolution raise or lower the standard of living of the majority of the British people?' 'What were the causes of the English Civil War in the seventeenth century?' 'What were the causes of the Second World War in the twentieth century?' 'Who killed the Princes in the Tower?'

Historians do disagree with each other. But then so, sometimes, do scientists. We must accept that all historical writing is in the end *interpretation,* that it must contain a subjective element (Unit 3, section 4). But this does not mean that 'one opinion is as good as another'. When you are reading history you must be always on guard against the crank or charlatan who claims to be putting forward a startling and imaginative new interpretation. If he has not observed the principles of scholarship outlined in this three-week *Introduction to History* then you have every right to reject his claims.

Similarly with your own writing. Imagination, the ability to penetrate behind the facts to the connections between them, is expected of you in any essay you write in humanities, but in a history essay you must be guided first of all by the information you have acquired from your various sources. There is all the difference in the world between creative historical *imagination* and sheer *invention* (that is, in this connection, simply making things up).

Two students, equally conscientious, equally able, may write entirely different essays on the same subject. Yet if both students have observed the basic principles of historical writing, both essays may be equally good. (It should be added that at student level the probability is that one essay will be more in accordance with historical reality as accepted by the leading historical authorities, and thus better as history.) Two historians, equally scholarly, may also present different conclusions on the same subject.

From what has already been said in *Introduction to History* the reasons for this should be clear to you.

EXERCISE

See how many of these reasons you can now recall, and see if you can add any further reasons of your own.

SPECIMEN ANSWER

1 History is always in some sense 'a dialogue between present and past' – every age rewrites history to take account of its own current preoccupations (see Unit 3, section 4) – thus a historian writing in 1977 will tend to present a different account from a historian writing in 1927.

2 The individual historian may believe to a greater or lesser degree in the possibility of establishing an underlying pattern of historical events. He may in general have a Marxist or a positivist outlook (Unit 3, section 6). He may believe in the possibility of building a 'model' for the discussion of such topics as industrialization (see discussion of Professor Flinn's 'model' in *The Nature of History*, pp. 230–1). On the other hand he may believe that 'things happen because they happen'; that history is just 'one damn thing after another'.

3 Greater or lesser use of modern 'scientific' techniques – e.g. statistics – can yield different conclusions.

4   The primary sources upon which history is based are usually fragmentary and imperfect and frequently conflict with each other so that historians studying the same evidence can still genuinely arrive at conflicting conclusions (Unit 4, section 6).

5   In the modern period the sources are so extensive that it may not be possible to consult all of them: different historians may consult different selections. They differ on which are the important data.

6   Even in other periods different historians may pay attention to different ranges of sources. Some historians might, for instance, pay little attention to place names or aerial photography.

To this list you may perhaps have thought of adding the following commonsense reasons for controversy and disagreement among historians:

7   Personality differences. One historian may tend to see human actions in an optimistic light, another in an entirely pessimistic light. For example, the first type of historian might present religion as a source of great inspiration to mankind, another might present it as simply a cause of bloodshed and atrocity.

8   A further related personality difference affecting historical writing is that between those who stress the importance of ideas in historical development, and those who stress economics. This difference might, for example, lead a historian of the first type to explain the American Revolution as a struggle for liberty, while a historian of the second type might represent the Revolution as basically a plot on the part of American merchants to feather their own nests. The fundamental tension in historical discussion between, on the one side, a stress on material developments, and, on the other, upon ideas, will figure prominently in the last third of this course, *Arts and Society in an Age of Industrialization*.

9   Political differences. A socialist, for example, may instinctively incline to the view that the industrial revolution had an adverse effect on the standard of living of the working classes, whereas a conservative might tend to take the opposite view, springing to the defence of the capitalist employers of the day. (Of course, a historian's biases do not necessarily undermine his argument.)

These nine reasons for the existence of controversy and disagreement among historians have simply been listed in the order in which they happen to have come up in this course, so far. Some historians would put more weight on some, other historians on others. Personally I (and I stress that this is only *my* opinion) think that the key to historical controversy lies in the fragmentary nature of historical evidence.

Two final reflections on the reasons for historical controversy. Sometimes historians do express their interpretation of a particular subject in rather more extreme terms than their own reading of the evidence would really allow for; there is, let us say, a natural tendency to make one's own point of view stand out as strongly as possible in contrast to one's predecessors and opponents. Likewise historians sometimes also form a personal emotional attachment to their own side of the argument – and so find it difficult to see the other point of view.

Controversy is a strong word. It implies more than just differences of interpretation among various historians. Rather it suggests that there are two or more schools of thought ranged against each other over the interpretation of a particular historical episode.

Disagreement, different opinions, we have seen, are inevitable. But should not historians play down their differences, instead of indulging in vigorous controversy of a type which sometimes verges upon personal attack?

In fact argument and debate, properly conducted, serve valuable purposes in all academic disciplines, history included.

EXERCISE

Have you any idea what these purposes might be? If you genuinely have no idea, don't bother to cudgel your brains, but go straight on to my answer.

Figure 8   Arnold Toynbee, 1852–83 (Radio Times Hulton Picture Library).

SPECIMEN ANSWER

1   Controversy can open up new lines of enquiry. The historian who has researched deeply into some problem can become blinded to the existence of wider perspectives and alternative lines of enquiry as he delves ever deeper into his subject. If his interpretations are boldly attacked by other historians then he will be forced to defend himself and to give consideration to the alternative interpretations forced upon him in the controversy. Out of all this the total sum of historical knowledge may be significantly increased.

2   It can lead to the critical testing of a particular generalization or hypothesis. Just as the detailed researcher can become blinded by his researches, so too the historian who has formulated sweeping generalizations or bold hypotheses can fall in love with his own theories and forget that every general formulation must be constantly re-examined in the light of new evidence. Controversy with another historian will force him to undertake this re-examination. Again the cause of historical knowledge may be advanced.

3   It can lead to new synthesis. An historical controversy may take the form of one hypothesis being posed against another. It may be that the historians concerned dig in their heels and refuse to modify their own hypothesis. Even so, a clear sharp statement of the conflicting theories may make it possible for other historians to present a *synthesis* which combines the best of each hypothesis, and in fact marks a definite advance in historical knowledge.

A number of problems or controversies in history are discussed in chapter VII of *The Nature of History.* You can see there how in some cases controversy has led to a general advance in historical knowledge. The whole area of Renaissance Studies is full of controversy and debate: you get hints of some of those debates as you read through Dickens (for example the relationship between politics and culture in Renaissance Florence (p. 14), or the precise nature and significance of economic development in the Renaissance period (p. 16)). One key theme at the heart of *The Age of Humanism and Reformation* is also a matter of some controversy: that is the idea of Renaissance humanism as an all pervasive school of thought influencing both the Reformation and all subsequent social and intellectual developments. Another leading British authority on the Renaissance, Professor Denys Hay has argued against the thesis that there is a direct causal link between Renaissance humanism and the Reformation, and he has, for example, stressed the mediaeval German origins of Lutheranism. Professor Hay (in contrast with Professor Dickens) has also argued that Renaissance ideas were not related to the rise of modern science.[1] Personally, I find Professor Dickens more persuasive on both points, but the issues are too complex to be discussed further here. Let us instead turn to that other area of powerful change (and of historical controversy): the Industrial Revolution.

[1]These views emerge most clearly in Denys Hay, *The Italian Renaissance in Its Historical Background* (1968).

Figure 9   Hans Baron.

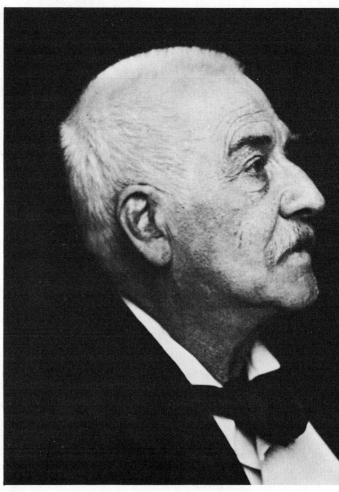

Figure 10   Jacob Burckhardt, 1818–97 (Universitäts-Bibliothek, Basel).

Figure 11 Friedrich Engels, 1820–95 (Photo by Debenham: Radio Times Hulton Picture Library).

EXERCISE

1   The passage quoted below is a rather extreme statement about the effects of
the Industrial Revolution which today most historians would not accept
without some qualification.

'Rome imported slaves to work in Italy: Englishmen counted it one of the
advantages of the slave trade that it discouraged the competition of British
colonists with British manufacturers . . .

'Yet England did not escape the penalty. For it was under this shadow that
the new industrial system took form and grew, and the immense power
with which invention had armed mankind was exercised at first under
conditions that reproduced the degradation of the slave trade . . .

'In adapting this new power to the satisfaction of its wants England could
not escape from the moral atmosphere of the slave trade: the atmosphere in
which it was the fashion to think of men as things . . .

'In the early nineteenth century the workers, as a class, were looked upon
as so much labour power to be used at the discretion of, and under conditions imposed by, their masters; not as men and women who are entitled
to some voice in the arrangements of their life and work . . .

'The needs of the London workhouses on the one hand, and those of the
factory on the other, created a situation painfully like the situation in the
West Indies. The Spanish employers in America wanted outside labour,
because the supply of native labour was deficient in quantity and quality.
The new cotton mills placed on streams in solitary districts were in the
same case. The inventions had found immense scope for child labour, and

145

in these districts there were only scattered populations. In the workhouses of large towns there was a quantity of child labour available for employment, that was even more powerless and passive in the hands of a master than the stolen negro, brought from his burning home to the hold of a British slave ship. Of these children it could be said, as it was said of the negroes, that their life at best was a hard one, and that their choice was often the choice between one kind of slavery and another. So the new industry which was to give the English people such immense power in the world borrowed at its origin from the methods of the American settlements.'

(a) Briefly set down any obvious subjective influences you detect in this passage.

(b) Yet, just because this passage is phrased so strongly it does clearly open up one rather interesting and possibly fruitful line of enquiry. What is that?

2   Now read this passage which presents a rather different interpretation of the Industrial Revolution.

'. . . It was through such changing seas that the captains of the industrial revolution steered their courses. Many of the difficulties they encountered were, it is clear, of their own making. Some of the navigators were unable to distinguish a false wind from a true, and not all knew when it was safe to clap on sail, or prudent to shorten it. Not all, again, took sufficient thought of the state of their crews: pioneers have often suffered disaster by reason of this. But the major troubles arose, not from want of skill or want of heart – certainly not from want of courage – but from the forces of Nature and the currents of political change. If harvests had been uniformly good; if statesmen had directed their attention to providing a stable standard of value and a proper medium of exchange; if there had been no wars to force up prices, raise rates of interest, and turn resources to destruction, the course of the industrial revolution would have been smoother, and its consequences would not have been, as they are, in dispute . . .

'An historian has written of "the disasters of the industrial revolution". If by this he means that the years 1760–1830 were darkened by wars and made cheerless by dearth, no objection can be made to the phrase. But if he means that the technical and economic changes were themselves the source of calamity the opinion is surely perverse. The central problem of the age was how to feed and clothe and employ generations of children outnumbering by far those of any earlier time. Ireland was faced by the same problem. Failing to solve it, she lost in the forties about a fifth of her people by emigration or starvation and disease. If England had remained a nation of cultivators and craftsmen, she could hardly have escaped the same fate, and, at best, the weight of a growing population must have pressed down the spring of her spirit. She was delivered, not by her rulers, but by those who, seeking no doubt their own narrow ends, had the wit and resource to devise new instruments of production and new methods of administering industry. There are today on the plains of India and China men and women, plague-ridden and hungry, living lives little better, to outward appearance, than those of the cattle that toil with them by day and share their places of sleep by night. Such Asiatic standards, and such unmechanised horrors, are the lot of those who increase their numbers without passing through an industrial revolution.'

What subjective influences do you detect here?

3   Write a *synthesis* of these two passages, i.e. a short passage of your own bringing together what you think are the best points made in each passage. 100–200 words will suffice.

Note: This exercise is designed purely to give you practice in writing, and, more important, to bring out the point that something positive can emerge from two opposed historical interpretations. It should be emphasized however that in writing a complete history essay it is not generally a good idea to try to balance out two opposed points of view: there are times when you will have to come down on one side or another, or establish a special point of view of your own.

SPECIMEN ANSWERS

1   (a) The author clearly has very deep sympathy for the 'workers' and strong hostility to the 'masters'.

In fact this is a passage from a book by J. L. and B. Hammond, who were at the head of the early twentieth-century tradition of left-wing denouncers of the evils of the Industrial Revolution (for more detail see *The Nature of History*, pp. 64 and 228).

(b) Apart from the broader point, made of course by many other historians, but driven home with great force here, that conditions during the industrial revolution *were* terrible, this passage suggests as a fruitful line of enquiry the connection between attitudes fostered by the slave trade and the tolerance of such bad conditions during the Industrial Revolution.

2   Clearly the author is very much on the side of the employers. In his references at the end to India and China he seems just as emotional as the Hammonds. He is in fact T. S. Ashton, the most distinguished of the economic historians who, in the inter-war years, reacted sharply against the Hammonds (see *The Nature of History*, pp. 230–1).

3   Undoubtedly conditions were harsh for the majority of the British people during the early stages of industrialization. Some employers were uncaring and quite happy to recreate what the Hammonds have called 'the moral atmosphere of the slave trade: the atmosphere in which it was the fashion to think of men as things'. Children were transported from the workhouses of large towns to the remote areas where cotton mills were being built. Yet not all the suffering was caused directly by the employers: dearth and destruction were caused too by the long period of wars with France, and by an unfortunate series of bad harvests. Arguably the majority of the British people, in a time of rapidly rising population, would have been much worse off had there been no industrial revolution to provide new sources of employment, food and clothing.

DISCUSSION

To build up this synthesis all I have done is to pick out what seem to be the most impressive points made by each writer, along with the one point (first sentence) which clearly emerges from both accounts: whatever the reasons, conditions undoubtedly were pretty harsh. The other points are:

1   From Ashton: *some* employers were uncaring (Ashton puts it in rather elaborate metaphorical style, suggesting perhaps that deep-down he feels he is on rather weak ground here: 'not all took sufficient thought of the state of their crews').

2   From the Hammonds: these employers anyway (though the Hammonds clearly thought them a majority) accepted the 'moral atmosphere of the slave trade' – strong words so best quoted directly in order to avoid any suggestion of plagiarism.

3   From the Hammonds: children transported from workhouses to cotton mills.

4   From Ashton: effects of war and bad harvests must be taken into account as well.

5   Ashton's final point: on balance, because of rising population, it is just as well that the Industrial Revolution did take place.

The final product is a fairly balanced account, which does not gloss over the obvious evils as Ashton tends to do; but which equally recognizes the achievements of the Industrial Revolution which the Hammonds rather ignore.

The Hammonds were writing before and just after the First World War; Ashton was writing before and just after the Second World War. Till the middle fifties the views put forward by Ashton, Clapham and others (see *The Nature of History*, pp. 228–9) tended to be dominant. More recently, however, historians with Marxist sympathies, in particular Professor E. J. Hobsbawm, have re-opened the debate. One of the most famous of all historical controversies in recent years has been that between Professor Hobsbawm, and Dr R. M. Hartwell, who took up the challenge from the more pro-capitalist position formerly occupied by Ashton and Clapham.

We cannot explore this controversy here either, though you will encounter it again when you come to Units 21–32.

9 HISTORY AND THE OTHER HUMANITIES

This is a humanities course, and these units, *Introduction to History*, form only a part of that course. To study most real problems (for example, Revolution, or Public Lending Right, or the Rights of Women) the tools and insights of one single discipline will never be enough for a really thorough analysis. (*Jane Eyre*, though it is many, many other things as well, is an important document in the study of women's rights: to study it effectively in this sense needs the skills, at least, of the philosopher and the historian, as well as those of the literary critic.) Furthermore one of the major aims of this Foundation Course is 'to raise questions about the possible relations between technological development, social organization, religion, thought and the arts'.

In fact this sort of discussion lies at the centre of the historian's activities since in general the historian would argue that in order to appreciate any work of thought, literature or art, it is essential to have some understanding of the state of technological development and social organization at the time the particular work was produced – in other words to understand its historical context. This is not to deny that the really important things about a piece of philosophy or a piece of art (the points that interest the philosopher, or the art critic) may have very little to do with the historical context; nor is it to deny the possibility that genius may exist entirely independently of any specific historical period. All the historian is saying is that our appreciation will be added to, perhaps only in a very minor way, by an understanding of the historical context.

Beyond that the historian is interested in discussing the relationship between political structure, economic conditions, etc. and works of art. But he does not pre-judge whether there is any direct connection between these things.

Again you will probably be familiar with books which make facile statements about particular works of art being 'products of their age' or about a particular artist being 'the mirror of his age'. These phrases may have a simple value in making a simple point; but in general we must be very careful about taking it for granted that there is some clear and definite connection between a particular historical context and a particular work of art. The best historical writing will seek to explore and analyse the infinitely subtle relations between social and historical factors and particular works of art.

EXERCISE

Reflect for a moment or two on what I have just said, then note down for yourself what you think to be the main ways in which history overlaps, or comes together with, or draws upon the other humanities.

SPECIMEN ANSWER AND DISCUSSION

So far I have really suggested three areas of overlap:

1 *Real problems* To study these in the round the various subjects have to come together.

2 *Context* The argument is that our appreciation of a painting, piece of philosophical writing, etc., will in some way be enhanced if we have an understanding of the historical context within which it was produced.

3 *Relationships* How do great works of art come to be produced? Perhaps we shall never know; but history has an important contribution to make to the discussion.

There is a fourth area which has already been discussed.

4 *Sources* Just as history can contribute to the study of literature, art, etc., so literature and art can contribute to the study of history.

Don't worry about the headings which I have italicized. These are just shorthand, convenience, expressions of my own: I don't expect you to have phrased things in exactly the same way.

In your reading of *The Age of Humanism and Reformation* you will have seen the extensive use Professor Dickens makes of artistic and literary sources (and you will learn more about his use of artistic sources in radio programme 5, *Art and the historian*).

If history can fit in as closely as this with the other subjects, is there any necessity to study history on its own (or for that matter any of the other subjects on their own)? Should we not, as some people argue, study man's experience as a whole, rather than splitting it up into its historical, literary, philosophical, etc., aspects? This is a big subject, well worth continuing to think about as you work your way through this Foundation Course in which we have chosen first to introduce the separate disciplines, then to try to bring them together. For the moment, I want to ask you this question.

EXERCISE

In what ways, if any, do you think that history *differs* from the other humanities? Again, if you are stumped, and time is running out, just imagine that you are sitting in a tutorial with me and I have asked a question which is too difficult for you to answer. Naturally I then give you my own answer – so please read on.

SPECIMEN ANSWER AND DISCUSSION

Well, I have already in Unit 3, Section 3 given a pretty full definition of history. Now, while there may be some overlap with other subjects contained within this definition, obviously it differs radically from definitions which will be given of the study of music, literature, etc. So where precisely do the differences lie? I would suggest that they are broadly two-fold.

1   Material studied.

2   Method of study.

1   Material
History is concerned with man's social and political activities. It is concerned with public events, relationships between groups in society, changes in these relationships, and with questions of causes, consequences and inter-relationships.

2   Method
Probably the point can be best illuminated, and brought most directly within your own experience, if one looks at the way one studies history compared with the way one studies other humanities' subjects. In literature there is a great deal of value to be derived from the study of one short poem, or one short play, such as *A Midsummer Night's Dream*. In art history there is a great deal of value in studying one or two paintings. In music one can study one single composition, in philosophy one short piece of philosophical exposition. The concern is with something inherent in these single artefacts themselves: questions of beauty, aesthetics, values, and so on. In history, there is little value in studying one single artefact in this way. You will often be asked to study one single historical document, but this will be as an exercise in historical method. You cannot learn much history from one document. The whole essence of historical study lies in the putting together of a large number of documents to build up a complete picture of an event, or of the relationships between events. 'Facts' in history are hard to establish, and do not quite have the nature suggested by that unfortunate method of school history teaching which presents the subject as a mere list of hard dates, kings, battles, etc. But in the end, it is possible and proper to

maintain that history is orientated towards facts, whereas the other humanities subjects are orientated towards values and aesthetic judgements.

However, I want now to turn to the positive question of the relationship of history to some of the other topics you will be studying in this Foundation Course. In the introductions to the other disciplines you will, among other things, be studying some of the arts and architecture of the Renaissance, the play *A Midsummer Night's Dream* by William Shakespeare, and some of the philosophical ideas of Descartes, Malebranche, Leibnitz, Spinoza and Locke. All of these fall within the broad period usually described as the Renaissance, the fourteenth, fifteenth and sixteenth centuries, with an extension into the seventeenth century (the period, of course, of Dickens's book, which has a postscript on the seventeenth century). To understand the origins of the Renaissance we need to go back to the fourteenth century, though most of the individuals mentioned later in the course fall into the latter parts of the period, Shakespeare's play belonging to the end of the sixteenth century, and all of the philosophers belonging to the seventeenth century.

The Age of Humanism and Reformation was deliberately chosen both to introduce you to historical writing, and to set the historical context for other topics. Now as you near the end of your three weeks' study of history I am going to repeat in slightly elaborated form the summary of the main changes taking place between the fourteenth and seventeenth centuries which I gave you right back at the beginning of these units (does that seem a terribly long time ago?!)

1   First of all there was the turning among intellectuals towards the classical wisdom of Ancient Greece and Ancient Rome. This is the absolute fundamental of the Renaissance as an intellectual and artistic movement. But this turning to the past had a liberating effect which led to discoveries and changes which went beyond the wisdom of the classics. The whole broad development, defined as humanism, was discussed, you will recall, very fully in Dickens's opening chapter.

2   Springing out of this, but linked also to the other changes, was a change in the way in which men thought about society and the world in which they lived, involving: (a) a new emphasis on man as a comprehensible being worthy of study, and on his real needs as distinct from the overarching theological concepts of the middle ages and (b) a change from the contemplative, passive, 'monastic' spirit to one which encouraged men to take an active part in economic and political life.

3   Again linked to both of these, we have the great changes in the styles of artistic and literary expression, so clearly seen in the great painters of the Italian Renaissance, and also in the plays of Shakespeare.

4   Thinking men of the time were actually aware of these intellectual and artistic changes, and themselves, one way or another, spoke of 'a Renaissance'. This belief, among intellectuals, is a special characteristic of the age.

5   Fifthly (and from the point of view of whole societies perhaps most significantly), there was a great expansion in trade and commerce, together with great changes and upheavals in the social structures of the various European countries: expressing this in a very shorthand fashion, one can say that feudalism slowly gave way to capitalism.

6   There were important technological developments, and a development of a whole new scientific outlook. Descartes was greatly influenced by contemporary Dutch science, and his mathematical discoveries, in turn, are an important part of the 'Scientific Revolution' of the seventeenth century, with which, in turn, can be associated Malebranche, Leibnitz and Spinoza.

7   The rapid spread of printing, invented in the fifteenth century, the great increase in lay education, and the widespread use of the vernacular languages (instead of Latin) added up to a great expansion in the possibilities of *communication*.

8 The fifteenth century onwards marked the beginning of the great age of European exploration and colonization.

9 A great split in Christendom (linked in a subtle way with the growth of humanism, well analysed by Dickens) took place in the early sixteenth century, followed by a long period of religious wars, and religious controversy (to which, again, thinkers like Descartes, Leibnitz and Spinoza are closely related).

10 There were important political changes: the Turkish Empire established its position in Eastern Europe, Russia began to emerge as a major Eastern Empire; above all, the nation state (best exemplified by France and England – but note the qualifications Dickens makes in the first section of chapter 2) now began to take its place as the most important political unit in modern European history.

Overall, then, the entire period from the fourteenth to the seventeenth century was one of major changes affecting all subsequent history, and also, in itself, one of great upheaval and controversy. It includes the Reformation and the religious wars, including, in the seventeenth century, the Thirty Years' War (1618–48) on the European continent; it includes, in England in the seventeenth century, the Civil War, which can be seen both as a product of religious controversy, and as a product of the deeper social and economic upheaval. But eventually, as Professor Dickens makes clear in his postscript, these conflicts gave way to a period of greater tranquillity and toleration towards the end of the seventeenth century; the period of the great English philosopher, John Locke.

It is, of course, a matter of some debate how far these four centuries can legitimately be taken together as belonging to one period, that of the Renaissance. The main content of Dickens's book in fact ends within the sixteenth century, though he tends to stress a developing humanism as the linking idea right through the whole period into the eighteenth century. Other historians would argue that with the seventeenth century a new period of change begins with the emphasis clearly on mathematics and empirical observation, rather than on the classics. However, in studying the past, rigid lines can never be drawn anywhere and it seems reasonable to take as our historical context for most of the figures you will be looking at in the first half of this entire Foundation Course the whole Renaissance and late Renaissance period.

9.1 A MIDSUMMER NIGHT'S DREAM BY WILLIAM SHAKESPEARE

In Units 6–8 *Introduction to Literature* you will, among other things, be studying Shakespeare's *A Midsummer Night's Dream*. It may possibly surprise you to know that nobody knows with *absolute certainty* exactly when Shakespeare wrote this play, or why. Non-historians are perhaps too little aware of how much about the past remains obscure, simply because of the lack of hard evidence.

Of course, we know that Shakespeare wrote the play during the reign of Queen Elizabeth, and know that Elizabethan England formed a part of late Renaissance Europe. Thus it is not too difficult to get a hold of the general historical background, the fundamental ideas and assumptions shared by Shakespeare and his contemporaries, and the major upheavals which impinged upon their lives: again I direct you towards Dickens's *The Age of Humanism and Reformation*, particularly pp. 240–3.

But when it comes to particular detail about Shakespeare and his plays, we are in an area of considerable controversy among scholars. A. L. Rowse, a distinguished Oxford historian, noted, perhaps, for pushing his own views rather hard has argued, with some reason I think, that it takes a trained historian fully conversant with all aspects of Elizabethan society, to produce a valid historical picture of Shakespeare's life. In his well-known biography, *William Shakespeare*, he gives a number of examples where he feels literary critics have gone wildly wrong through lack of knowledge of Elizabethan history. There is agreement among scholars that the play was written in the 1590s, in the first instance for private presentation at a wedding ceremony, though later performed, with slight alterations, on the London stage. Rowse argues that the occasion was in fact the wedding in May 1594 of the widowed Countess of Southampton to Sir Thomas Heneage, twenty years her senior, and a confidential servant of the Queen. Rowse also argues that the famous lines

> To live a barren sister all your life,
> Chanting faint hymns to the cold fruitless moon . . .

do not refer to Queen Elizabeth, but to the Countess's son who had resolutely refused to get married.

But let us not get too bogged down in details. The sort of questions about the context of the play, and the influences on it, of interest both to the student of history and the student of literature are: how far can this meaningfully be described as a Renaissance play? How far an Elizabethan play? What economic, or other reasons, did Shakespeare have for writing this particular play at this particular time?

And you could say that (if you had the knowledge!) it is a Renaissance play, directly in the humanist tradition, in that Shakespeare draws upon English translations of such classical works as Plutarch's *Lives*, Ovid, and Apuleius's *Golden Ass*.

Where the play is of central interest to the historian is in the handling of the village artisans and craftsmen, and of their beliefs and superstitions. Here we have both a reflection of, and a source for, the village life, and beliefs, of Elizabethan England; though, of course, much care and subtle analysis is needed – how far, one might ask, was Shakespeare simply propagating the myth of 'Merry England'?

9.2   HISTORY AND PHILOSOPHY

I have argued, that in studying, say, the philosophy of Descartes, it can be helpful to know something of the historical context in which Descartes was writing, the intellectual and social preconceptions of his time, and so on. This is one obvious way in which the study of history overlaps with the study of philosophy. Essentially, in discussing the historical context of a piece of philosophical writing, one is approaching philosophy historically. But equally there is an overlap in looking at history philosophically. It can indeed be argued (and has been argued by my colleague Oswald Hanfling) that in raising some of the sorts of questions I have been discussing in these three units I have essentially been performing a philosophical, rather than a historical task. Actually, no philosopher of history, as far as I know, has ever analysed the basic purposes and methods of historical study in the way I have done (though it is also fair to say that very few, if any, historians have done so either). Philosophers of history, in practice, have concerned themselves with rather larger issues.

In this sub-section I am going to refer very briefly to two rather different types of philosophy of history, which, in fact, coincide with the two rather different definitions of 'history' which you encountered right at the very beginning of these units.

EXERCISE

Remind yourself of what these two broad uses of the word 'history' are, and from that deduce what the two different types of philosophy of history must be.

Figure 12   G. W. F. Hegel, 1770–1831. Portrait by Jakob von Schlesinger (Mansell Collection).

Figure 13   Professor A. J. Toynbee, 1889–1975 (Camera Press: Photo: Tom Blau).

SPECIMEN ANSWER

History as the past, and history as the historian's attempt to reconstruct and interpret that past. The first type of philosophy of history concerns itself with seeking meaning or intelligibility in the past itself; it is concerned with history as a process that goes on independently of the puny activities of the working historian. The second type of philosophy of history is concerned, as I have been in these units, with the actual activities of the historian himself; however, instead of being content as I have been with a simple account of what practising historians actually do, such philosophers set out to ask questions about the nature of historical knowledge and to assess the general validity of the sort of explanations historians offer of historical events. The philosopher is in a position, as I am not, to compare the historians' activities with those to be found in other branches of knowledge.

I shall start with the first type of philosophy of history, one which, quite frankly, is now very much out of fashion. Indeed, I would argue that attempts to produce grand theories about history as process are very much the products of a particular historical period centring in the early nineteenth century. Here, indeed, we are back to our first type of overlap, which will pop up again when you study the early nineteenth century at the end of this course. You will then encounter the German philosopher Georg Wilhelm Friedrich Hegel (1770–1831).

Hegel was responsible for applying Plato's notion of 'the dialectic' to history. This meant that to Hegel each age would be characterized by dominant ideas of a certain type – the 'thesis'. But the age must also contain within in it exactly

154

contradictory ideas – the 'antithesis'. 'Antithesis' working against 'thesis' would ultimately produce a 'synthesis' – the predominating ideas of a new age.

In seeking the fundamental meaning of the historical process, Hegel found it in 'the development of the consciousness of freedom' (since Hegel was an extreme conservative, and an employee of the autocratic Prussian state we may note that his idea of freedom was not exactly ours). Hegel detected a progression from the despotism and slavery of the Oriental world, to the citizenship rights of the Greek or Roman world, to the individual liberties of the Germanic nations (note: not Prussia alone) of the Europe of his day. The basis of the progression, of course, was the dialectic, the process of 'thesis', 'antithesis' and 'synthesis'. History (the past), then, is a grand design unfolding in four stages, Oriental, Greek, Roman and Germanic; and Hegel believed he could establish the special characteristics of the people or nation dominating each stage in his historical development. Finally, Hegel saw such 'great men' as Caesar or Alexander as chosen instruments in bringing about the unfolding of this grand design.

The dialectic, we have seen, was taken over by Marx, though 'turned upside down' so as to apply to material developments not ideas. Marxism (another product of the nineteenth century), too, falls in part into the category of grand theorizing about history as a process, save that Marxism, as we also saw, has provided practical tools for working historians.

Grand-scale theorizing about history has been out of fashion in the twentieth century, where the emphasis has been on detailed empirical study combined with a general scepticism about grand designs in history or anything else. At this point you might well expect me to discuss Professor A. J. Toynbee's[1] *A Study of History* (vols. 1–3, 1934; vols. 4–6, 1939; vols. 7–10, 1954) which is certainly grand design history aimed at revealing some of the general laws behind the rise and decline of civilizations. But whatever else Toynbee was not, he was certainly not a philosopher (as Hegel was); and thus it is not strictly relevant to bring him in here (if you are interested, you can read about Toynbee in *The Nature of History* pp. 83–7).

So I must move quickly to the central issue which concerns philosophers of history writing today, the debate over the nature of historical knowledge and the status of historical explanation. From meeting Open University students at summer school and elsewhere, I know that many of you are fascinated by this topic. Others of you, perhaps, couldn't care less. If you fall into this latter category *you are entirely at liberty to cut the rest of this section and go straight to my Conclusion on page 162.* Anyway, all I have time to do here is to broadly indicate the three main positions in the debate, and refer you to some of the leading authorities and the books they have written, in case you should wish to take the matter further, and perhaps make it a subject of discussion once you get to summer school. For those of you who are interested I apologize for the brevity of the treatment and for any other deficiencies arising from the fact that I am not myself a trained philosopher.

1   The position that historical explanation must conform to the logical structure observed in other branches of knowledge, particularly the natural sciences, and involving reference to a general law. This is usually referred to as 'The Popper-Hempel thesis' or as 'The Covering Law thesis'. Carl G. Hempel first published his famous and much-quoted article 'The Function of General Laws in History' in 1942. It has been reprinted in several collections of readings on philosophy of history, including Patrick Gardiner (ed), *Theories of History* (1959), pp. 344–6. There are other essays by Hempel in William H. Dray (ed), *Philosophical Analysis and History* (1966), and Sydney Hook (ed), *Philosophy and History: A Symposium* (1963). As a fairly quick route to the basic views of Sir Karl Popper you could read K. R. Popper, 'Prediction and Prophecy in the Social Sciences' in Gardiner, *Theories of*

---

[1]The nephew of the Arnold Toynbee who coined the phrase 'the Industrial Revolution'.

History, or, if you are *very* keen *The Logic of Scientific Discovery* (1959). The *Poverty of Historicism* (1957) is in large measure a polemical attack on Marxism.

2 The position that history is an entirely 'autonomous' branch of knowledge with a logic of explanation entirely of its own.

(a) One of the most distinguished exponents of this view was R. G. Collingwood (1889–1943), who combined his Professorship of Philosophy at Oxford with a lectureship in history (where he specialized in Roman Britain). Collingwood set out to release history from what he called its 'state of pupillage to natural science'. He argued that whereas the scientist is concerned with the 'outside' of events, the historian must endeavour to penetrate to the 'inside' and 'rediscover' the thoughts of their agent. 'All history' says Collingwood, 'is the history of thought.' The historian discerns these thoughts 'by rethinking them in his own mind'. The essential task of the historian is 'the re-enactment of past thought in the historian's own mind'. The simplest introduction to Collingwood's ideas is to be found in his own historical association pamphlet, *The Philosophy of History*, published in 1930. His *The Idea of History*, published after his death, is a much more complex and subtle work. For a very bare summary you could turn to *The Nature of History*, pages 79–83 – though I am afraid it is true to say that these pages betray my own impatience with Collingwood's ideas.

(b) A slightly different defence of the autonomy of history has been presented by Professor Michael Oakeshott, for many years a prominent political philosopher at the London School of Economics. Oakeshott simply denied that it was possible (or necessary!) to establish historical explanation as explanation in terms of cause and effect. Oakeshott likened the historian's activities to those of the novelist, arguing that narrative in history, as in a novel, provides all the explanation required.

3 Various intermediate positions.

(a) A number of philosophers have argued that, without accepting the Collingwood thesis in full, it can be shown that the Popper–Hempel thesis is not applicable to history. You could turn to one or other of the collections of readings already mentioned, and look at contributions by William Dray, A. C. Danto, W. B. Gallie and Alan Donagan.

(b) The argument which sees historical explanation as generally different from, yet sharing common ground with, scientific explanation. This argument has been put forward most impressively in two books which probably come nearest to expressing what professional historians themselves believe about these problems of historical explanation: Patrick Gardiner's *The Nature of Historical Explanation* (1952) which, while demonstrating that the 'regularity' explanation of natural science is not the only valid form of explanation, strongly criticizes the arguments for the autonomy of history presented by Collingwood and Oakeshott, and concludes with a view of historical explanation as different from, yet as sharing important points in common with, scientific explanation; and W. H. Walsh's *An Introduction to the Philosophy of History* (1951 and 1967) which concludes:

> Our general view can be summarized by saying that history is, in our view, a form of knowledge with features peculiar to itself, though it is not so different from natural science or even common sense as it has sometimes been thought to be.

As I have said very few practising historians have in fact engaged in dialogue with the philosophers of history. One of the most outstanding exceptions is Professor G. R. Elton whose work on Tudor England we have already briefly encountered. Elton makes himself out to be a firm believer in the autonomy of historical study. The arguments of 'the Popper–Hempel school or of those who fall back on symbolic logic' he sees as 'quite mistaken'. Yet Elton in his key work, *The Practice of History* (1967), has no time for Collingwood either:

This unreal and unrealistic notion that the historian understands history by reenacting it in his mind, backed up by the fatal suggestion that ideas are the only realities in history, has had some very disturbing consequences, from the conviction that no history is worth writing except intellectual history to the opinion that history is just what the historian dreams up.

Elton is grateful for the efforts of Gardiner, Dray, Danto, Gallie and Donagan but he fears that in laying to rest the Popper–Hempel thesis they run the risk of resurrecting the ghost of Collingwood and suggesting that in the end historical explanation does depend very heavily on the historian's own intuition. Elton is keen to establish that just because historical explanation does not depend upon universal laws, that does not mean that it is not governed by very strict rules – which, of course, is what I too have been trying to establish during the course of these units. Elton argues that these philosophers of history have too often based their conclusions on rather brief excerpts from historical writing (and often not very good examples at that); he maintains that the philosophers need to study much more thoroughly all the activities that go in to the production of a piece of historical writing. Elton also deals with Oakeshott's idea, taken up by Professor Gallie, that the telling of the story itself contains the historical explanation. This, he says, 'underestimates the difficult complexity of explaining by narrating. In order to explain, narrative needs to contain a great deal of explicit analysis and argument, difficult to write.' This, of course, chimes exactly with what I said in section 3.

Elton sums up the nature of historical causation and the historian's explanation as follows: 'Direct causes explain why the event actually happened; situational causes explain why direct causes proved effective and why the event occupies a particular place in the historical picture and story, both as an effect and as a cause of further effect.'

In company with most professional historians, I am in broad agreement with the views presented by Professor Elton, though I would not take such a hard, conservative line on the question of the autonomy of history, which, in any case, does not in my view follow necessarily from Professor Elton's arguments. An even more conservative line is taken in the somewhat idiosyncratic *The History Primer* (1971) by the distinguished American historian of seventeenth-century England, J. H. Hexter. Avowedly this sets out to refute Hempel, and, by examples of what the historian actually does, returns to a position of full autonomy for historical explanation. Hexter is highly amusing, but not in my view, completely persuasive.

Such works as *The Historian's Craft* by Marc Bloch, *What is History?* by E. H. Carr, *The Aims of History* by David Thomson and *The Death of the Past* by J. H. Plumb are stimulating and illuminating personal testimonies, rather than systematic philosophies of history. In fact there is no real rival to Gordon Leff's *History and Social Theory* (1969), a comprehensive and elegant work by an historian whose specialism, significantly, is the History of Thought. Leff puts great stress (as I have done) on the fragmentary and imperfect nature of historical sources. Unlike Elton he does not believe that the historian can establish distinct 'direct' and 'situational' causes. He puts a stress above all upon contingency in history – hence there cannot possibly be any general laws. The fundamental conceptualizing activity of the historian, Leff maintains (and again I agree) is periodization (see section 7).

To round off this discussion I want to add my own conviction that many of the difficulties in regard to philosophical attempts to explain what historians are doing arise, first (as Leff stresses) from the fragmentary nature of historical sources, and, second, from the very complexity of the problems which historians set themselves. We have already seen that the Reformation is a relatively straightforward concept when compared with say 'Humanism' or 'the Counter-Reformation', and, most certainly, when compared with the concept of 'the Renaissance'. When dealing with the Renaissance it is very difficult indeed to devise a clear cause and effect model because that which has to be explained, the Renaissance, is in itself a very difficult and complex 'effect' to pin down. Some of my own researches have been concerned with the social consequences of the Second World War. It is not enough to say, as Elton does, that this simply involves moving the cause and effect model further forward, that the effect is now the social consequences, and the cause is the war. In fact the question of whether there were any substantial social consequences of the Second World War is a matter of considerable debate among historians: so my problem is not just one of showing an acceptable cause and effect relationship, but of demonstrating that the effect exists in the first place (the 'cause', on the other hand, indisputably does exist!). But in case even the enthusiasts among you have now got too terribly muddled, let me stress again that this section is not intended to do more than raise questions which you may wish to return to in later parts of the course.

The controversy over the social effects of World War II. You learned something of this controversy in television programme 3, Writing History. Now study Figures 14–19 and ask yourselves what light, if any, they throw on this topic.

Figure 14   Hunger March, 1936 (Radio Times Hulton Picture Library).

Figures 15 and 16   Children being evacuated during World War II (Camera Press, London).

Figure 17 Coventry blitz, 1940 (Times Newspapers Ltd).

Figure 18 Civil servants in Blackpool, 1943 (Photo from Cmnd. 7955 Report of the Ministry of National Insurance. *Reproduced by permission of the Controller of Her Majesty's Stationery Office).*

Figure 19   *Elephant and Castle, 1945 (Radio Times Hulton Picture Library).*

10 CONCLUSION: EVALUATING HISTORY AND HISTORIANS

If you have mastered the material discussed during the last three weeks, you should now be much better able:

(a) to read history (that is to say, although you are aware that there are bound to be differences of opinion and controversies among historians, you now have a basic idea of how to judge whether one historian is more worth paying attention to than another);

(b) to write history (that is to say, given sufficient basic information, you should be able to *plan* and, later in the course, to write a short history essay – for the next few weeks we shall continue to concentrate on getting you to write short answers. Your essays will differ from those of other students doing this course, and, of course, different interpretations can be perfectly acceptable, but you now appreciate that there are also basic principles upon which your tutor can decide whether one essay is better – more historical, more true to how things actually did happen – than another.)

Here is a checklist of the points which have come up during the last three weeks, against which you can evaluate: (a) books by historians (and would-be historians), and (b) your own essays.

1 Depending on the level of communication the historian is aiming at (monograph, pop history, student essay, etc.) he should have made efficient and critical use of all the sources available to him. His work should, in this sense, be scientific.

2 Again depending upon the readership aimed at, the historian should communicate his information in a clear and efficient manner. At best his manner of presentation should conform to the highest canons of literary style, showing that history is art as well as science.

3 Depending on the subject of study, and bearing in mind that history is concerned both with change through time and with explanation and interconnections, he should establish a reasonable balance between narrative, analysis and description.

4 He should seek always to be concrete and precise and to steer clear of the dangers involved in (a) periodization, (b) relating art etc. to historical context, and (c) historical semantics.

5 History should not be propaganda. Grosser subjective influences should always be eliminated. Yet historical writing often derives an extra quality from the special point of view of the author. Completely objective history is an impossibility.

UAA - DON'T FORGET   *Oswald Hanfling*

Please have Units 2B and 9 handy for this section.

'Simple men', wrote Sir Francis Bacon, 'admire them; and wise men use them'. Bacon was writing about studies.[1] He went on: 'for they teach not their own use.' This very true of Units 2B and 9, *Uses and Abuses of Argument* (UAA). There is no point in studying those units unless you *use* what you have learnt there in your reading and writing elsewhere. But this is not something that is guaranteed just by working through that material. It needs to be kept alive by alertness and constant practice. To give you such practice we are including a regular UAA feature in each block of the A101 course. These features will be quite short, and I hope you will enjoy working through them. Here is the first.

Imagine you are a course tutor marking a history assignment, and bearing in mind the points made in Units 2B and 9, Part 1. The assignment is given below and what I would like you to do is to criticize certain words and phrases in it. The question is taken from Unit 5 section 4, and so is most of what the student has written. (Well – actually I wrote it myself!) However, to do this exercise you do *not* need to check whether the student has 'got his facts right'. The criticisms I have in mind can be made purely by examining the assignment itself. I would like you to look out for the following:

Rash generalization (see UAA, page 14).

Doubtful meaning (see UAA, section 2.1 – discussion of extracts *C*, *E* and *H* – pages 16, 17 and 20).

Hyperbole (see UAA, page 21).

'Persuader-words' (see UAA, section 2.3).

'Crafty conflation' – or just muddled conflation (see UAA, section 2.5).

Question-beggers (see UAA, section 2.6).

'You can't win' (see UAA, page 34).

An important point made by Arthur Marwick in the first paragraph of section 4 of Unit 5.

What I would like you to do is this. Underline or circle the offending words and phrases in the assignment and write your 'tutor's comments' in the margin of page 164. You might write things like 'What is this word doing here?', 'Do you mean . . . or . . .?', 'This phrase takes for granted that . . .', 'What you say is too general – perhaps in *some* cases it is true that . . .', 'Aren't you conflating . . . with . . .?', 'Is this relevant?'

My own answer is given in two stages. First the assignment is reproduced on page 165 and there I have merely marked the relevant words and phrases. Please check your answers against this and revise them where appropriate. Then turn to page 166 where there is a further reprint with my own 'tutor's comments' added.

---

[1] In his essay 'Of Studies'. Bacon's *Essays* were first published in 1597.

'Did Western Europe in the sixteenth and seventeenth centuries achieve greater economic prosperity and attain a higher level of intellectual and cultural activity than Western Europe in the previous two centuries?'

The history of the sixteenth and seventeenth centuries, apart from being interesting in itself, can greatly contribute to an understanding of our own society.

The fact that Western Europe was better off and culturally more advanced in the sixteenth and seventeenth centuries than ever before can be explained in a number of ways. Throughout the period the people of Europe were conscious of living in a new age. Italy saw the emergence of the High Renaissance – surely an advance on anything that had been achieved before. The works of such men as Sir Thomas More and Erasmus were certainly unique, and had few parallels in the preceding centuries. No one who is able to appreciate works of art would deny that the paintings of Rembrandt, Claude and Poussin are superior to those of the preceding centuries. There was a flowering of High Renaissance architecture in Italy, though it must be admitted that in the other countries no architectural achievements took place.

In the field of literature we have to remember that Shakespeare and Milton lived in the period, and that nothing comparable to their writings had been produced in earlier centuries. Moreover, it can be said that the writings of these authors were definitely modern.

The invention of printing obviously provided new opportunities for the spread of ideas, though it is impossible for us to judge the quality of what was actually printed.

It is no wonder that the seventeenth century has been called 'the age of reason'. The great scientific discoveries of Galileo and others brought about an emphasis on science, or reason, which had not been known in the previous centuries. This emphasis on reason was bound to mean a greater degree of tolerance of other people's views.

The new age of science did not, however, bring about a reduction in superstition: religious belief remained as strong as ever.

In spite of the Civil War, England saw a growth of economic prosperity; thus the mass of the people were better off. Similarly, the Dutch embarked on a golden age of discovery and colonization.

All in all, it is undeniable that the sixteenth and seventeenth centuries heralded a new era of cultural achievement and economic prosperity.

'Did Western Europe in the sixteenth and seventeenth centuries achieve greater economic prosperity and attain a higher level of intellectual and cultural activity than Western Europe in the previous two centuries?'

The history of the sixteenth and seventeenth centuries, apart from being interesting in itself, can greatly contribute to an understanding of our own society.

The fact that Western Europe was better off and culturally more advanced in the sixteenth and seventeenth centuries than ever before can be explained in a number of ways. Throughout the period the people of Europe were conscious of living in a new age. Italy saw the emergence of the High Renaissance – surely an advance on anything that had been achieved before. The works of such men as Sir Thomas More and Erasmus were certainly unique and had few parallels in the preceding centuries. No one who is able to appreciate works of art would deny that the paintings of Rembrandt, Claude and Poussin are superior to those of the preceding centuries. There was a flowering of High Renaissance architecture in Italy, though it must be admitted that in the other countries no architectural achievements took place.

In the field of literature we have to remember that Shakespeare and Milton lived in the period, and that nothing comparable to their writings had been produced in earlier centuries. Moreover, it can be said that the writings of these authors were definitely modern.

The invention of printing obviously provided new opportunities for the spread of ideas, though it is impossible for us to judge the quality of what was actually printed.

It is no wonder that the seventeenth century has been called 'the age of reason'. The great scientific discoveries of Galileo and others brought about an emphasis on science, or reason, which had not been known in the previous centuries. This emphasis on reason was bound to mean a greater degree of tolerance of other people's views.

The new age of science did not, however, bring about a reduction in superstition: religious belief remained as strong as ever.

In spite of the Civil War, England saw a growth of economic prosperity: thus the mass of the people were better off. Similarly, the Dutch embarked on a golden age of discovery and colonization.

All in all, it is undeniable that the sixteenth and seventeenth centuries heralded a new era of cultural achievement and economic prosperity.

Have you compared your answers with my markings, shown above? I hope they correspond to a large extent, but of course there are likely to be quite a few differences. I could easily have marked some other words and phrases, and put my comments in other ways, stressing different aspects etc. When you are ready, read on and compare our comments.

'Did Western Europe in the sixteenth and seventeenth centuries achieve greater economic prosperity and attain a higher level of intellectual and cultural activity than Western Europe in the previous two centuries?'

Is this relevant to the question?

The history of the sixteenth and seventeenth centuries, apart from being interesting in itself, can greatly contribute to an understanding of our own society.

Now you are *begging* the question (Please look at the question again).

The fact that Western Europe was better off and culturally more advanced in the sixteenth and seventeenth centuries than ever before can be explained in a number of ways. Throughout the period the people of Europe were conscious of living in a new age. Italy saw the emergence of the High Renaissance – surely an advance on anything that had been achieved before. The works of such men as Sir Thomas More and Erasmus were certainly unique and had few parallels in the preceding centuries. No one who is able to appreciate works of art would deny that the paintings of Rembrandt, Claude and Poussin are superior to those of the preceding centuries. There was a flowering of High Renaissance architecture in Italy, though it must be admitted that in the other countries no architectural achievements took place.

All of it? All of them? (This statement is too general.)

What does 'surely' contribute here?
A rash generalization.

Be careful with hyperbole. Doesn't 'unique' mean *no* parallels?
Does this mean that anyone who disagrees with you must be unable to appreciate art?

This again is too general.

You take for granted that what follows is *true*. (This is OK for 'lived in the period', but not for the rest of what you say.)
How do you mean? Comparable in which way?

In the field of literature we have to remember that Shakespeare and Milton lived in the period, and that nothing comparable to their writings had been produced in earlier centuries. Moreover, it can be said that the writings of these authors were definitely modern.

What does this mean? Modern from whose point of view?

This is too sweeping. (No doubt there would be *some* difficulties about it.)

The invention of printing obviously provided new opportunities for the spread of ideas, though it is impossible for us to judge the quality of what was actually printed.

It is no wonder that the seventeenth century has been called 'the age of reason'. The great scientific discoveries of Galileo and others brought about an emphasis on science, or reason, which had not been known in the previous centuries. This emphasis on reason was bound to mean a greater degree of tolerance of other people's views.

Why do you conflate these words? (*Which* was unemphasized in earlier times?)

Why? Do 'reason' and 'tolerance' mean much the same?

Why do you conflate these words? Couldn't there be religious belief *without* superstition?

The new age of science did not, however, bring about a reduction in superstition: religious belief remained as strong as ever.

166

Why 'thus'? Do these things mean more or less the same? (Couldn't the mass of the people have remained poor?) Why 'similarly'? (Again you are conflating different things.)
Is it really undeniable? (Or is this word meant to *persuade* the reader?)
Consider what this word means. Are you now writing about *later* centuries?

In spite of the Civil War, England saw a growth of economic prosperity; thus the mass of the people were better off. (Similarly,) the Dutch embarked on a golden age of discovery and colonization.

All in all, it is undeniable that the sixteenth and seventeenth centuries heralded a new era of cultural achievement and economic prosperity.

Notes

1   I didn't object to 'obviously' in the paragraph about printing, because it seems to me that that really is obvious.

2   I hope you spotted the point from Arthur Marwick's section, in my list of things to look out for. (See my first comment on the assignment.)

3   As I said before, don't worry if you marked some things differently from my answer. You may perhaps have picked out more generalizations than I did. This is a fault that runs through the assignment as a whole, for example in lumping together the two centuries, contrary to the layout suggested in Arthur Marwick's specimen answer.

4   Alan Foster, a tutor who made many valuable comments on my drafts of UAA, added a 'General criticism' at the end of this assignment. He wrote: 'A very *vague* answer with words of doubtful meaning ("the people of Europe", "new age", "superior", "flowering" '); and pointed out that this criticism applied to the assignment in general and could not properly be confined to particular words and phrases. I quite agree. Evidently writing bad assignments is something I am good at!

ACKNOWLEDGEMENTS

The comments of Open University students and tutors have been invaluable in preparing this completely new version of *Introduction to History*. Arthur Marwick would also like to express his special thanks for the constructive comments of John Ferguson, Oswald Hanfling, Rosalind Hursthouse, Anne Duckworth, Christopher Harvie and Ellie Mace.

Grateful thanks are also given to the following for use of Figures 32–35 (pages 94–6): Figures 32 and 33, Museum of London; Figure 34, Photo John Freeman; Corporation of London Records Office; Figure 35, Windsor Collection; reproduced by gracious permission of Her Majesty the Queen.